GETTING ANGRY
SIX TIMES A WEEK

GETTING ANGRY
SIX TIMES A WEEK

A PORTFOLIO
OF POLITICAL CARTOONS

14 MAJOR CARTOONISTS

edited with an introduction by
ALAN F. WESTIN

profiles by
ALBERT ROBBINS
and
RANDALL ROTHENBERG

BEACON PRESS   **BOSTON**

e following:

The Milwaukee Journal. Re-
and The Milwaukee Journal.
?, 74, 75, 76, 77, 78 by Jules

76, 77, 78, 79 by Michael
Keete. Reprinted by permission of The Denver Post.
Don Wright cartoons: Copyright © 1979 by Don Wright. Reprinted
by permission of Don Wright.
Paul Szep cartoons: Copyright © by Paul Szep. Reprinted by permis-
sion of The Boston Globe.
Ben Sargent cartoons: Copyright © 1979 by The Austin American-
Statesman. Reprinted by permission of The Austin American-
Statesman.
Doug Marlette cartoons: Copyright © by The Charlotte Observer.
Reprinted by permission of Doug Marlette.
Bill Mauldin cartoons: By permission of Bill Mauldin and Wil-Go
Associates, Inc. Copyright © 1967, 71, 72, 76, 77, 78.
Mike Peters cartoons: Copyright © 1977, 78, 79 by Mike Peters and
Dayton Daily News. Reprinted by permission of Dayton Daily News.
Paul Conrad cartoons: Copyright © 1972, 75, 76, 77, 78, Los Angeles
Times. Reprinted by permission.
Tony Auth cartoons: Copyright © 1976, 77, 78 by The Philadelphia
Inquirer, The Washington Post Writers Group. Reprinted by per-
mission of Tony Auth.
Hugh Haynie cartoons: Copyright © 1977, 78 by The Courier-Journal.
Reprinted by permission.
P. B. Oliphant cartoons: Copyright © 1975, 76, 77, Los Angeles Times
Syndicate, The Washington Star, Oliphant. Reprinted by permis-
sion of The Washington Star.
Draper Hill cartoons: Page 156—Copyright © by The Commercial
Appeal. Reprinted by permission of The Commercial Appeal.
Pages 157–160—Copyright © 1979 by The Detroit News, dis-
tributed by King Features Syndicate. Reprinted by permission.

Beacon Press books are published under the auspices
of the Unitarian Universalist Association
Published simultaneously in Canada by
Fitzhenry & Whiteside Limited, Toronto
Printed in the United States of America

(hardcover) 9 8 7 6 5 4 3 2 1
(paperback) 9 8 7 6 5 4 3 2 1

Library of Congress Cataloging in Publication Data

Main entry under title:

Getting angry six times a week.

1. United States—Politics and government—1945-
—Caricatures and cartoons. 2. Civil rights—United
States—Caricatures and cartoons. 3. Cartoonists—
United States—Biography. I. Westin, Alan F.
E839.5.G43 1979   741.5'973   79-51553
ISBN 0–8070–4378–8
ISBN 0–8070–4379–6 pbk.

CONTENTS

Introduction   vii
ALAN F. WESTIN

This Is What the Bill of Rights Is All About   1
BILL SANDERS

Up against the Wall!   13
JULES FEIFFER

What Gives Me the Right to Make These Comments?   27
MIKE KEEFE

Hitting between the Eyes Every Day   37
DON WRIGHT

I Have a Bent for Satire   49
PAUL SZEP

A Mindset of Absolute Irreverence   61
BEN SARGENT

Things Were Much Worse Than I Ever Expected   73
DOUG MARLETTE

I Don't Like to See Uncommon Men Suppressed   85
BILL MAULDIN

A Good Cartoonist Is like a Loaded Gun   95
MIKE PETERS

The Constitution Is a Hell of a Document   105
PAUL CONRAD

Confronting People with What They Don't Want to See   115
TONY AUTH

Getting Angry Six Times a Week   127
HUGH HAYNIE

Sometimes I Lash Out at Both Sides   139
PAT OLIPHANT

I Try to Forget That I've Ever Read Histories   151
DRAPER HILL

INTRODUCTION

ALAN F. WESTIN

Political cartooning has a long, stormy, and utterly fascinating history. In their lively account of American political cartooning, *The Ungentlemanly Art*,[1] Stephen Hess and Milton Kaplan observe that cartoonists have been at work "ever since some stone-age Herblock scratched an irreverent representation of a tribal chief on his cave wall." The oldest surviving political caricature is believed by some scholars to be a nasty drawing of King Tutankamen's father, done in 1360 B.C. This would create a 2300-year line of artistic succession to the cartoonists who drew nasty pictures of Richard M. Nixon in the 1970s.

Political cartooning is not only an ancient art form but also one in which the great practitioners in the United States and abroad have been powerful intellectual and political forces in their times. William Hogarth's savage lithographs exposed the exploitation and misery of the poor in eighteenth-century London. Honoré Daumier laid bare the hypocrisy of lawyers and doctors in early nineteenth-century France and rallied the forces of liberal nationalism. During World War I, the Allied cause was powerfully aided by the anti-Hun cartoons of the Dutch artist Louis Raemaekers, while a similar role in World War II was played by the great anti-Nazi cartoonist in England, David Low.

In the United States, amateur artist Benjamin Franklin exemplified the early American tradition when he drew the famous cartoon that showed the colonies as separate pieces of a serpent that must "Join or Die." The "middle period" of American cartooning saw caricaturist Thomas Nast drive Boss Tweed and his Tammany Ring from power in New York City in the 1870s with what Boss Tweed lamented as "those damn pictures!" From the Civil War until the end of World War II, American political cartooning flowered with great practitioners such as Frederick Opper, Homer Davenport, Joseph Keppler, Rollin Kirby, Clifford Berryman, Jay N. Darling, and Daniel Fitzpatrick.

1. Stephen Hess and Milton Kaplan, *The Ungentlemanly Art* (New York: MacMillan, 1968).

Today, both in numbers of artists and in public impact, and despite the awesome role of television in the news process, we are in a golden age of political cartooning. Draper Hill, the cartoonist historian, estimated that there are over 150 full-time editorial cartoonists drawing today for newspapers and magazines, with "at least forty to fifty nationally well known." And, in what explains the appearance of this collection, Draper Hill observes that "civil liberties have now become a weekly staple of today's cartoonists, not just a once-in-a-while topic."

This was not always the case, nor is the generally pro-civil liberties direction of today's editorial cartooning the way it was during the pre–World War II eras of political caricature. Therein lies a story worth telling.

From the colonial days of etching, broadside, and placard down to the present, political cartoons have had several consistent elements. They have generally been comments on specific political issues or personalities of the day, usually tied to very concrete events. Most cartoonists in each era, drawing as they did and still do for expensive and established media, have reflected the dominant social and political attitudes of the day, with only a small minority offering radical ideas, usually in the "offbeat" publications of each era.

Recognizing these continuing aspects, how were civil liberties treated in the years between the creation of the American Republic and the current era? First of all, late eighteenth- and early nineteenth-century American cartoons often featured highly stylized and allegorical treatments. Lithographs and broadsides showed the Constitution and Bill of Rights being safeguarded from tyranny, a toga-wearing Miss Liberty being assaulted by various treacherous political figures or native American Republicanism fighting off European despotism. This tradition was nicely illustrated in the classic work *A Century of Political Cartoons: Caricature in the United States from 1800 to 1900*,[2] by Allan Nevins and Frank Weitenkampf, which reproduces and discusses 100 representative cartoons of this period. They show, for example, a famous anonymous drawing in 1800 whose Federalist sentiments depicted Thomas Jefferson being prevented by an American eagle clutching the Constitution from sacrificing "American liberty" on an "Altar to Gallic Despotism" (the French Revolutionary regime).

By the 1840s, cartoons had become more skillful in both

2. Allan Nevins and Frank Weitenkampf, *A Century of Political Cartoons: Caricature in the United States from 1800 to 1900* (New York: Scribners, 1944).

portraiture and the communication of political ideas. In 1848, one celebrated cartoon lambasted the action of South Carolina and other slave states in refusing to allow free discussion of the "slave question." As Nevins and Weitenkampf describe the background, "Through the South freedom of assemblage, freedom of speech, and freedom of the press were rigidly restricted. The right of petition, the free use of the mails, and in some instances the right of jury trial were denied. These invasions of fundamental Anglo-Saxon liberties, with repeated instances of mob violence, converted many fair-minded Northerners to an anti-slavery position." One response was a lithograph cartoon published in New York called "Joshua Commanding the Sun to Stand Still." It showed the South Carolina political leader John C. Calhoun pointing to a small printing press in the sky designed to look like a sun and announcing these words (in the traditional balloon over the speaker's head): "Sun of intellectual light and liberty, stand ye still, in masterly inactivity, that the Nation of Carolina may continue to hold negroes and plant cotton till the day of Judgment!"

As our two examples suggest, political cartoons, then as now, invoked the symbols and sentiments of liberty to advance viewpoints of the cartoonists (and their publishers) that ranged all across the political spectrum of each era. This can be illustrated by two famous cartoons during the early decades of the Republican Party. The first, drawn by Louis Maurer in 1856 and issued by Currier and Ives, portrayed the presidential candidate of the new Republican Party, John C. Fremont, as a leader of all the radical groups of the day. In "The Great Republican Reform Party Calling on Their Candidate," Maurer lined up the following suitors pressing their demands on Fremont:

a gaudily attired, overdressed black man at the head of the line, declaring, "De Poppylation ob color comes in first— arter dat, you may do wot you pleases."

a Catholic priest holding a cross and saying, "We look to you, Sir, to place the power of the Pope on a firm footing in this country."

a spry spinster, petition in hand, inviting Fremont "to the next meeting of our Free Love association, where the shackles of marriage are not tolerated and perfect Freedom exists in love matters and you will be sure to enjoy yourself, for we are all Freemounters."

a tramplike working man, unkempt and with a liquor bottle clutched in his hand, announcing: "An equal division of property is what I go in for."

a representative of the Woman's Rights movement, smoking a cigar, carrying a horsewhip, and dressed in the liberationist clothes advocated by Amelia Bloomer, making her demand for "the recognition of Women as the equal of man with a right to vote and hold Office."

and last, a tall, thin representative of the Prohibitionist movement, saying, "The first thing we want is a law making the use of Tobacco, Animal Food, and Lager-bier a Capital Crime."

A decade later, after secession had been put down by civil war, Currier and Ives published a cartoon in 1868 that portrayed the Republican Party and Negroes in a very different fashion. In "Reconstruction, or 'A White Man's Government,'" the cartoon showed a white Southerner in plumed hat being swept down a raging river toward a rock-strewn waterfall. A Negro man, now handsomely depicted, is on the shore, holding on to the "Tree of Liberty" with one hand for support and holding out his other hand to save the Southerner. "Give me your hand, master. Now that I have got a good hold on this tree I can help you out of your trouble." The Southerner, refusing, replies: "You go to thunder! Do you think I'll let an infernal Nigger take Me by the hand? No sir-ree, this is a white man's government." To which President Ulysses S. Grant, standing back on the shore and watching this scene, comments to the Southerner: "My friend, I think you had better use all means to get ashore; even if it is a black man that saves you."

Though examples of cartoons can be found in the nineteenth century supporting free expression, Negro rights, women's suffrage, or civil rights of workers, the mainstream of American political cartooning in this era was overwhelmingly hostile to the civil liberties claims of such groups. "To the end of the nineteenth century," Nevins and Weitenkampf record, "no sharply radical notes were struck by the major cartoonists." Women's rights advocates were generally lampooned as absurd; minority religious groups (notably Catholics and Jews) were treated with a contempt that reflected dominant anti-Semitic and anti-Catholic bias; after the end of Reconstruction, Negroes came to be treated as inferior children, through Southern eyes; cartoons became more and more hostile to recent immigrants, especially Asiatics and Eastern Europeans; and movements of social protest such as Populism or the Knights of Labor were portrayed as a wild collection of barn-burners and agitators. "All this was natural enough," Nevins and Weitenkampf observed, "for America was a conservative country" in this period.

In the first half of the twentieth century, the thrust of political cartooning in the press was not much better as to civil liberties and civil rights. While some leading cartoonists attacked the trusts, political corruption, and exploitation of labor in the first two decades of the twentieth century and the 1930s saw some liberal cartoonists emerge to defend New Deal reforms and labor unions, the center of gravity of American political cartooning was still profoundly conservative. There was the minority—and eloquent—work of artists such as Rollin Kirby in the New York *World Telegram,* Daniel Fitzpatrick in the St. Louis *Post-Dispatch,* or Edmund Duffy in the Baltimore *Sun.* There were also occasional cartoons in the main press against lynching, the Klan, and other outrages in the name of white supremacy, or attacks on the most extreme suppressions of free speech (such as Boss Hague's ban on political meetings in Jersey City in the 1930s). But it was only in the small radical or foreign-language press that cartoonists such as Art Young, Robert Minor, and William Gropper would consistently and often attack denials of rights of expression, association, and elementary justice to those challenging the antilabor, segregationist, and exploitive institutions of those times. Also, in terms of supporting wartime limitations on civil liberties, almost all cartoonists in the general press adopted "patriotic" positions during World Wars I and II, leaving the tiny radical press to provide cartoons of dissent and pacifism.

An important point to appreciate was that, before the 1940s, the primary thrust of American constitutional law as defined by the Supreme Court was profoundly conservative. From John Marshall's day through the New Deal era, down to the "switch in time that saves nine" in 1937, rights of political expression and dissent, procedural due process for accused persons, and rights of racial and sexual equality rarely prevailed in the High Court. The Constitution and the Bill of Rights and the Civil War amendments primarily served the rights of property, liberty of contract, and employer prerogatives. Those who appealed to the law of the land to protect liberty usually appealed to the law as they wished it should be, not as the Supreme Court ruled that it was. For every new civil liberties decision of the Supreme Court in the 1900–1945 years, there were five or ten times the number of decisions rejecting civil liberties and civil rights claims. As a result, most cartoonists of those days reflected prevailing notions when they adopted very limited concepts of rights.

After World War II, especially during the cold war loyalty-security days of the forties, most editorial cartoonists for the national press and magazines reflected dominant public opinions and drew pictures justifying loyalty oaths, blacklists, political surveillance, FBI wiretapping, library censorship, and other assaults on constitutional rights in the name of anti-Communism. Only a handful of luminous exceptions, such as Fitzpatrick, Bill Mauldin, and Herblock (Herbert Block), con-sistently cartooned against such measures. And it was only when the excesses of Senator Joseph McCarthy and the begin-nings of detente with the Soviet Union changed the political climate that many cartoonists in the 1950s adopted more pro-civil liberties positions. On the Negro equality front, however, specifically on the practices of Jim Crow in the South, the mainstream of American political cartoonists in the forties and fifties (outside the South) adopted strongly pro-civil rights positions. Their cartoons against racial segregation con-tributed some of the most eloquent political commentaries of those decades.

The sixties and seventies saw political cartooning in the mass media grow increasingly pro-civil liberties. In part, this re-flected broadening popular acceptance of these values; in part, it stemmed from the fact that civil liberties and civil rights actions—or inactions—were now the staple of daily political events and debates that cartoonists could comment on with relish. Still another factor was that a whole new generation of political cartoonists arrived who were strangers to the cold war era of 1947–1960. They came of age in the turbulent politics of the civil rights, antiwar, and student-protest movements of the 1960s and early '70s. These young cartoonists, with anti-establishment outlooks and counterculture styles, joined the ranks of the Herblocks and Mauldins and helped make cartoons about civil liberties and civil rights the steady diet of editorial drawing that they are now.

It was in recognition of the vitality and importance of civil liberties commentary by leading cartoonists that The Civil Liberties Review, an independent bimonthly national magazine begun in 1973 and sponsored by the American Civil Liberties Union, began its Cartoon Gallery in the spring of 1977. Each issue of the *Review* after that time featured a profile and a representative selection of civil liberties cartoons by one of the country's leading cartoonists.

By early 1979, the *Review* had published ten such Galleries. They presented the work of Doug Marlette of the Charlotte *Observer*, Don Wright of the Miami *News*, Tony Auth of the Philadelphia *Inquirer*, Mike Peters of the Dayton *Daily News*, Ben Sargent of the Austin *American-Statesman*, Pat Oliphant of the Washington *Star*, Hugh Haynie of the Louisville *Courier-Journal*, Paul Szep of the Boston *Globe*, Jules Feiffer of the *Village Voice*, and Herbert Block (Herblock) of the Washington *Post*. Another half-dozen cartoonists had been lined up as the willing subjects of future Galleries.

At that point, however, *The Civil Liberties Review* had to be closed for financial reasons by the ACLU, and independent funds to keep it going could not be raised. Rather than see the cartoon Galleries lost to a wider readership, we decided to write the profiles and collect the cartoons of the other cartoonists who had agreed to be featured and to publish all the Galleries in a book of political cartoons about civil liberties.[3] The additional cartoonists included Bill Mauldin of the Chicago *Sun-Times*, Draper Hill of the Detroit *News*, Paul Conrad of the Los Angeles *Times*, Bill Sanders of the Milwaukee *Journal*, and Mike Keefe of the Denver *Post*. We regret that we were unable to use the cartoons of Herblock, who has been an eloquent and powerful voice for civil liberties longer than any American cartoonist still at work.

The fourteen cartoonists whose work appears within are all staunch supporters of civil liberties. They range in age from thirty to near-sixty, in education from high school dropout to Ph.D., in background from military officer to conscientious objector. Bill Mauldin made his career choice in 1935; Mike Keefe didn't make his until 1975. Bill Sanders uses light humor to get a point across; Paul Conrad prefers devastating force. Paul Szep and Draper Hill count British caricaturist David Low as their major influence; Hugh Haynie points to Herblock as his, and Tony Auth to Ronald Searle.

In one respect, our group is incontrovertibly alike: they are all male, and they are all white. Perhaps there is no good

3. The profiles for the cartoonists whose work appeared in the *Review* were written, from personal interviews, by *CLR*'s Managing Editor in 1977–1978, Albert Robbins. The additional profiles were done by *CLR* Staff Editor Randall Rothenberg, with the exception of the profile of Paul Szep, which was written by *CLR*'s book review editor, Stephen Salisbury.

reason for this, other than the fact that the field has been dominated by white males for such a long time that it has been difficult for women and minorities to break in. It may also be that the visibility of the daily cartoonist's output has made editors afraid to give women and minorities a chance to express their political views. But even this may be changing; recently, Long Island's *Newsday*, one of New York City's leading suburban newspapers, hired M. G. Lord to take over the daily artistic editorial. Ms. Lord showed her mettle when, in the space provided for "Wife's Name" on an Association of American Editorial Cartoonists' questionnaire, she wrote "Are such things necessary?"

While our fourteen cartoonists are unquestionably in favor of civil liberties, and such is the raison d'être for their being in this book, they express a variety of opinions when matters of civil liberties definition, strategy, and tactics arise, or when one claim to liberty collides with another. Paul Conrad's antiabortion stance has infuriated California feminists who otherwise receive strong support for women's rights from the cartoonist. Bill Mauldin considers himself to be a balancing force to "gun-control fanatics." Pat Oliphant won his 1967 Pulitzer Prize for a cartoon many perceived to be pro-war.

Nevertheless, these cartoonists speak with one voice on many current civil liberties issues. For example, they are strongly for freedom of the press, and strongly against police and intelligence agency abuses; strongly in favor of safeguards to privacy, and strongly against the civil liberties violations of the Nixon administration.

Incidentally, lest it seem to be neglected through oversight, these fourteen men also have one paramount element in common: they are devastatingly funny. Their caricatures and situations raise smiles, laughs, whoops, and angry surprise, and that is what makes them among the great cartoonists of our era, whatever their topic of the moment and the viewpoint they adopt. We are, indeed, a better society and our rights are more secure because these artists do "get angry six times a week."

Alan F. Westin

GETTING ANGRY
SIX TIMES A WEEK

THIS IS WHAT
THE BILL OF RIGHTS
IS ALL ABOUT

BILL SANDERS

Bill Sanders has participated in his share of controversy. There was, for instance, the time he attended a Milwaukee mayor's press conference dressed as Colonel Sanders of Kentucky Fried Chicken fame. And the time the Milwaukee *Journal* slapped him with a two-week suspension for cartooning for an underground newspaper. Most recently, on the day a Sanders cartoon appeared depicting a Wisconsin judge in a ticklish situation with a young lady in an elevator, the judge checked into a hospital suffering from "exhaustion."

"It's not that I say, 'Hey, today I'm going to be controversial,' " says the forty-seven-year-old Sanders. "I just believe that life is too short not to enjoy, and not meaningful if you don't have certain commitments to act upon."

Sanders has taken his love of humor, penchant for controversy, and firm belief in civil liberties and combined them to become one of the best-known editorial cartoonists in the country. His awards from groups as diverse as the National Collegiate Athletic Association and the Milwaukee Civil Liberties Union attest that his efforts have not gone unrecognized. Those efforts would have been difficult to ignore anyway: from the time he joined the *Journal* in 1967 until recently, his cartoons appeared every day on the front page, and they have been widely reprinted in the national media.

Sanders, whose work the *Saturday Review* claimed "can make the opposition gag on its breakfast" did not peg himself for this line of work early. By his own admission, he was a "dumb jock" in college. Although modesty prevents him from detailing his accomplishments, a little digging reveals that Western Kentucky State College quarterback "Whitey" Sanders set an NCAA passing record during his senior year. With an ROTC commitment to fulfill, he entered the army, assuming he'd spend a couple of years there before playing pro football.

"I played some ball down at Fort Benning, and then went overseas to Korea," recalls Sanders. "I remember thinking, 'Boy, there's an awful lot going on in the world,' and I ran into some interesting people. One of them was this private, a graduate of a small eastern college, and bright as hell. He really helped to expand my consciousness, 'cause he kept saying, 'Well, how do you *really* feel about that?' "

As luck would have it, Lieutenant Sanders was made officer in charge of *Stars & Stripes* in Korea, running a printing plant and a six-man news bureau. His lack of experience in a field that excited him moved him to do a bit of research. "One day I was in the base library, and I picked up a Herblock book. That just blew my mind, to draw, and to say things the way he said them—I guess it was at that point I said, 'That's what I would like to do.'"

Taking his separation from the army, Sanders—no longer contemplating a gridiron career—remained in the Orient, finding employment as a general assignment reporter on *Pacific Stars & Stripes,* a quasi-service newspaper. Soon he began serving in a dual role as sportswriter and cartoonist, and also free-lanced for the Japan *Times* drawing political cartoons. His first stateside job was with the Greensboro, North Carolina, *Daily News,* and in 1963 he moved to the Kansas City *Star.* By that time Sanders had hit his stride, as evidenced by the fact that the local John Birch Society campaigned—unsuccessfully—to cancel 10,000 *Star* subscriptions because of Sanders' attacks on them.

The emotional reaction to Sanders' work has continued during his twelve years in Wisconsin, and the cartoonist himself best describes the reasons. "I have done a lot of cartoons on abortion, gay rights, women's rights—in specific areas of real, live social issues, that people get very on edge about. I feel strongly that these situations are the parameters of social rights, that these are what the Bill of Rights is all about. It makes people uncomfortable."

His readers are also made uncomfortable, he believes, because he doesn't hesitate to depict real characters in compromising situations. "I try to be as specific as possible in dealing with people who have their hands on the levers of power."

To Sanders, the CIA is not a cloaked individual stealthily sneaking around corners, it is a Frankenstein monster breaking down doors and crushing innocents. Walter Mondale, spared the barbs of most cartoonists and commentators, is depicted by Sanders as a stooge parroting administration dicta. In his own area, Sanders managed to enrage Milwaukee Mayor Henry Maier so much by the Kentucky Fried Chicken incident (which Sanders claims was provoked by Maier's insults) that the mayor issued a ban on press-conference attendance in costume. The cartoonist's campaign against municipal court judge Christ T. Seraphim (who, wrote Sanders, "used to take his first name seriously and the Bill of Rights in vain") has regaled *Journal* readers for years.

On the other side are the dogmatic radical "crazies" of the University of Wisconsin, who provided Sanders with the fodder for his popular cartoon series "Jack Radical, Anti-Amerikan Boy." Sanders' belief that Wisconsin is an "extremely lively state politically" would seem to be a mild understatement.

The cartoonist notes that, over the years, his tolerance for anti-civil libertarianism has decreased, "particularly when religious philosophy is used in the political arena."

"It's very prominent in this area," he says. "Lots of Lutherans and Catholics, powerful politically, and I'm just tired of these people setting the parameters of my behavior in the political system. Why, for a long while, until the ACLU got it knocked down, birth control devices were legally defined as indecent articles and could not be advertised. That was because of the religious lobby. In areas like sex education, abortion, birth control, school transportation—it's a kind of principled thing that begins to gnaw at you."

On the other hand, the cartoonist admits that he has mellowed over the years. "I guess I don't try to shoot from the hip quite as much as I used to," he says.

That may be so, but he continues to shoot with deadly accuracy at the misuse of power, and remains one of the most consistent civil liberties defenders in the cartoonist community.

'Wouldn't you prefer to leave your pets outside, Mr. Rehnquist?'

'Now I suppose there will be a big push to disclose more of this vital data to the general public!'

'I don't know what you chicks are complaining about. We're just trying to protect your feminine mystique.'

"I don't think they're interested in colored beads anymore."

*'What is ye worlde coming to? Allowing a
woman to control her own body!'*

'And to the Pasadena, Tex., school superintendent, our
Attila The Hun All Heart Award for suspending a 5
year old boy who wore long hair to cover a birth defect.'

'We operate on the general premise that you're guilty
until proven innocent.'

'Listen! I'm not gonna risk inciting some innocent judge into molesting me because of my provocative dress!'

'Quit whining about constitutional rights, kid! The US Supreme Court says you don't have any—where this is concerned!'

'The Supreme Court gave me this paper for us to read.'

'Remember when this used to be a stairway?'

UP AGAINST THE WALL!

JULES FEIFFER

"**O**utside of basic intelligence," Jules Feiffer told a Georgia audience last year, "there is nothing more important to a good political cartoonist than ill will. Cartoons are more likely to be effective when the artist's attitude is hostile, to be even better when his attitude is rage, and when he reaches hate he can really get going."

Feiffer has maintained all these attitudes steadfastly for over twenty years, mixing and matching them as fits the occasion, not only in his weekly cartoons for *The Village Voice,* but in plays like *Little Murders* and *The White House Murder Case,* films such as *Carnal Knowledge,* and in novels like *Harry, the Rat with Women.* In all these literary forms, he has been eminently successful in portraying the foibles, fears, and frustrations of middle-class Americans and the society that oppresses and bewilders them daily.

"I try to turn logic on its ear," says Feiffer, explaining his artistic method. "I take the suppositions of the people I'm disagreeing with to their logical but ridiculous extremes, and try to show how these arguments fail. And through that, I give the reader not just an opinion or an attitude, but a perception of what's really going on."

While Feiffer does attack the standard adversaries—reactionary politicians, orthodox business moguls, and anti-civil libertarians, for instance—he does not spare his erstwhile compatriots: Liberal and radical hypocrisies are displayed in all their smarmy glory. Feiffer is as comfortable going after enemies of the free press as he is in attacking what he calls the "liberal institutionalization of racism." Nor does he restrict himself to events and issues; emotions and philosophies are just as likely to come under Feiffer's scrutiny.

"The difference between other cartoonists and myself is a combination of form and politics," he says. "Basically, my belief is that everything is politics—fucking, schooling, everything. I've always dealt with the issues of language and power which combine to make politics—the politics of private life, of families, of the establishment."

Although he claims always to have been a political person, Feiffer refers to his time in the army as the point at which his singular cartooning career took form. Prior to his 1951 induction, he had been leaning toward a more orthodox comic-book cartooning life; he had assisted Will Eisner, who drew "The Spirit," and briefly drew his own syndicated cartoon, "Clifford." Then he was drafted.

"The army was my first direct contact with open fascism," recalls Feiffer. "It really propelled me into the world of satire, as a way of expiating my grief and rage. One either went crazy, or found a way to deal with it."

Feiffer's way of dealing with it was to begin work on "Munro," a cartoon story about a four-year-old boy who gets drafted by mistake. "Munro," which the artist calls his "first functional piece of satire," was later turned into an Academy Award–winning animated short subject.

Completing his hitch, Feiffer lived alternately on unemployment "and the six months of work it took to be eligible for unemployment. I always managed to get fired and do the work I cared about." That work was an early form of his well-known weekly cartoon, undeveloped and, he says, "wildly uncommercial at the time."

"Feiffer," the cartoon he began drawing gratis for the fledgling *Village Voice* in 1956, is eminently commercial these days. The chaotic skew-line is perfectly suited for detailing the anxieties of modern life and politics. "He is at war with complacency," wrote Russell Lynes, "with the cliché mongers who provide society with meaningless slogans to live by."

But to call Jules Feiffer a cartoonist is like calling Leonardo da Vinci a painter: It barely does justice to his work. Feiffer is artist, playwright, novelist, and political commentator. And the ill will, hostility, rage, and hatred that he prizes in his cartooning are evident in his plays and novels as well. Curiously, he backed into writing. Bored with cartooning and owing *Playboy* $5000 for undelivered work, he decided to take care of the debt by dashing off some stories. The result was his first novel, *Harry, the Rat with Women,* and a new career. A few years later he tried playwriting and discovered that he had a facility with it. Today, he says, "I find if I'm not doing both writing and cartooning, I don't really want to be doing anything."

Feiffer is ardently political personally as well as professionally. Aside from drawing on political matters, he has written pamphlets, spoken before various rights groups, and campaigned actively with organizations such as the ACLU and the National Committee for a Sane Nuclear Policy. This has brought a certain amount of criticism, which disturbs him not a bit.

"I've always been willing to be politically active, to lend my name or to associate directly with particular issues," says Feiffer. "A lot of people in the press disagree with this type of stance. They believe you have to retain a certain amount of distance—even Art Buchwald is of that opinion. But the work has no distance. Why the hell should I personally have distance on issues I clearly associate myself with in the work?"

Among the issues are civil liberties questions. "My interest in civil liberties is not with the subject per se, but how against the grain of the American character and the American orthodoxy the Bill of Rights is. Our better instincts, our instinct for self-preservation, makes us honor civil liberties, even though philosophically and in our hearts we would deplore them. It's our ambivalence toward civil liberties, the contradictions, that interests me."

Feiffer admits that he is worried, "but not actively," about recent negative trends in American attitudes toward civil liberties. He will not, however, change his method of attacking the problem, "which is to explain things to myself, and thereby the reader." Nevertheless, he encourages others to enter the fray.

"It seems to me that what we need at this moment in our history is a campaign to sell the Bill of Rights to the people it was created for," Jules Feiffer told an ACLU convention last year. "That there is a place in their lives for a free press, despite its distortions and special relationships; that there is a place in their lives for free speech, despite how outrageous or just plain disagreeable or wrong others who practice it may be; and that, despite the fact that civil liberties often prove to be unpleasant, inconvenient, and even painful, still they are of momentous value and make enormous practical sense."

I BELIEVE OBSCENITY IS A MATTER OF LOCAL COMMUNITY STANDARDS.

IN MY COMMUNITY YOU MAY GO WITH A GIRL FROM THE COMMUNITY AS LONG AS YOU DON'T FOOL AROUND WITH HER.

YOU MAY ONLY FOOL AROUND WITH GIRLS FROM OUTSIDE THE COMMUNITY.

YOU BREAK OFF WITH GIRLS YOU FOOL AROUND WITH AS SOON AS YOU FINISH WITH THEM SO YOU DON'T GET STUCK.

YOU MARRY ONLY A GIRL WHO NOBODY'S FOOLED AROUND WITH, AND YOU FOOL AROUND WITH HER TO THE EXTENT SHE EXPECTS IT—

AND STOP AS SOON AS POSSIBLE.

BUT YOU'RE ALLOWED TO FOOL AROUND ON BUSINESS TRIPS BECAUSE YOU'RE ALONE AND, ACCORDINGLY, FREE TO HAVE A GOOD TIME.

IF YOU DON'T APPROVE OF MY COMMUNITY STANDARDS, YOU CAN ALWAYS MOVE INTO A MORE LAX COMMUNITY.

IF YOU DON'T OBJECT TO BEING OBSCENE.

© 1974 JULES FEIFFER

I USED THE FREEDOM OF INFORMATION ACT TO WRITE IN AND GET MY F.B.I. DOSSIER.

IT SAYS: OCT. 12, 1966. PICKED UP GIRL AT CIVIL RIGHTS DEMONSTRATION. STRUCK OUT.

FEB. 3, 1967. PICKED UP GIRL ON PEACE MARCH. STRUCK OUT.

APRIL 10, 1968. PICKED UP GIRL AT McCARTHY RALLY. STRUCK OUT.

©1976 Jules Feiffer 2-15

NOV. 5, 1972. TRIED TO PICK UP GIRL AT WOMEN'S LIBERATION CONFERENCE. WAS DRIVEN FROM HALL.

NO MORE POLITICS.

YEAR AFTER YEAR OF SEXUAL HUMILIATION AND ITS ALL IN THE FILES

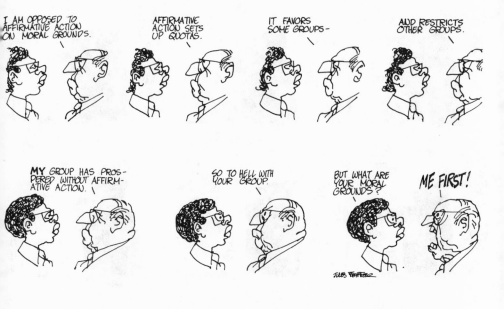

I AM OPPOSED TO AFFIRMATIVE ACTION ON MORAL GROUNDS.

AFFIRMATIVE ACTION SETS UP QUOTAS.

IT FAVORS SOME GROUPS—

AND RESTRICTS OTHER GROUPS.

MY GROUP HAS PROSPERED WITHOUT AFFIRMATIVE ACTION.

SO TO HELL WITH YOUR GROUP.

BUT WHAT ARE YOUR MORAL GROUNDS?

ME FIRST!

JULES FEIFFER

WE ARE NOT TERRORISTS. WE ARE FREEDOM FIGHTERS.

YOU ARE NOT **OUR** HOSTAGES. YOU ARE HOSTAGES TO IMPERIALISM.

JULES ORKFEIFFER

IF THE IMPERIALISTS DEFY THE PEOPLES' WILL THEY WILL BE RESPONSIBLE FOR YOUR DEATHS.

IF THE IMPERIALISTS BOW TO OUR DEMANDS YOU WILL BE RELEASED.

IF WE KILL YOU, THEY ARE YOUR MURDERERS. IF WE FREE YOU, WE ARE YOUR LIBERATORS.

OUR NEXT CLASS IN "REVOLUTIONARY COMMUNICATION" IS SCHEDULED FOR NOON, UNLESS WE BLOW YOU UP FIRST.

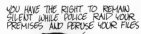

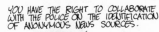

UP AGAINST THE WALL, NEWS- PAPER

THIS IS YOUR SUPREME COURT EDITING YOUR FIRST AMEND- MENT RIGHTS.

YOU HAVE THE RIGHT TO REMAIN SILENT WHILE POLICE RAID YOUR PREMISES AND PERUSE YOUR FILES.

YOU HAVE THE RIGHT TO COLLABORATE WITH THE POLICE ON THE IDENTIFICATION OF ANONYMOUS NEWS SOURCES.

YOU HAVE THE RIGHT TO STAY OUT OF TROUBLE BY STAYING ON THE GOVERN- MENT'S SIDE.

OH, I GET IT!

YOU WANT ME TO GO BACK TO PRE- VIETNAM NEWS COVERAGE—

AND SUPPRESS THE NEWS VOLUN- TARILY

MY BOY!

©1978 JULES FEIFFER

THE TERM "HUMAN RIGHTS" DEMANDS CLARIFI- CATION.

BY "HUMAN RIGHTS" I DO NOT MEAN LIBERAL, SIMPLISTIC, IRRESPON- SIBLE "HUMAN RIGHTS."

WHAT I MEAN BY "HUMAN RIGHTS" IS COMPETENT, MANAGERIAL, ZERO-BASE BUDGETED "HUMAN RIGHTS."

AS OPPOSED TO DIS- RUPTIVE AND UN- HELPFUL "HUMAN RIGHTS."

SO I WOULD ADVISE OUR CITIZENS TO BE SURE THAT THEY SUPPORT **QUALIFIED** "HUMAN RIGHTS"—

FOR VERIFICATION, PLEASE CHECK WITH ME CY VANCE OR THE SHAH OF IRAN.

©1978 JULES FEIFFER

WHAT GIVES ME THE RIGHT TO MAKE THESE COMMENTS?

MIKE KEEFE

Can a mild-mannered, Midwestern college mathematics professor find happiness as an editorial cartoonist in Rocky Mountain country? Mike Keefe may be the only person in history to make that transition, but judging from his success at it, other budding Euclids should be encouraged. After three and a half years at the Denver *Post,* he still marvels at his situation.

"I get paid to know what's happening—that's the fun part about this job," says Keefe. "That's something a lot of people would like to have time to do, and I think it's a wonderful way to live. I can't know everything that's happening, but it is kind of nice to have an overview of the world."

The thirty-two-year-old Keefe didn't always have that overview. In fact, before landing the job at the *Post* he was "stuck in an ivory tower situation," studying for his Ph.D. in math at the University of Missouri and teaching at a community college in Kansas City. Although he enjoyed his studies, the realities of the market forced him to look elsewhere for survival.

"I had a good academic background, and good grades, and sent applications to about two hundred schools," recalls Keefe. "I didn't get a nibble—the market was completely flooded. About then I decided, well, maybe I ought to start pushing this hobby of mine, doing political cartoons."

Keefe admits now that his decision to change careers may have spring from plain naiveté. Had he known how tight the job market was for cartoonists, he would probably have set his sights on another line of work. For, unlike a Bill Mauldin or a Mike Peters—cartoonists who had been drawing since early childhood—Mike Keefe picked up his hobby in graduate school: "I mostly doodled in the margins of math papers—not much more than that." This advanced to the stage where he drew a weekly cartoon for the college newspaper. On a whim, he send some examples of his work to Bill Sanders in Milwaukee, whose material Keefe had come to know when the older cartoonist was at the Kansas City *Star.* Sanders forwarded it to the *Post,* and the rest is recent, if continually evolving, history.

As with cartooning, Keefe came to political awareness late in life. He was in the Marines, and the catalyst for him was an event few in his generation will ever forget.

"I had been hitchhiking around the country, after a few years of college, and got drafted at twenty-three, which was pretty old, spent part of the time at Camp Pendleton, and at Puget Sound, and had orders to go to Vietnam twice. Anyway, I was just interested in having a good time, and didn't necessarily want to be in the Marines, but I didn't think they were all that bad in the beginning.

"Then, in the spring of nineteen seventy, Kent State happened. I was in a Marine barracks with a bunch of MPs at the time, and those Marines—they were siding with the National Guard: 'Kill those fucking hippies.' That just shocked me, the whole incident shocked me. But the fact that I was right in the center of a group of people who were with the wrong side really upset me. I began to pay more attention to what was going on."

Working for the Denver *Post,* the paper that first propelled Paul Conrad to national prominence, and following directly on the heels of Pat Oliphant, Keefe says he was rather intimidated by that newspaper's proud heritage of political cartooning. He also believes his "greenness" allowed the *Post* "to put their thumb on me a little bit" in the beginning, and prevented him from immediately establishing a political and artistic style. He places the break-point at about a year ago. His drawing developed when he decided to use plain white paper, eschewing the gray-toned graphics of most cartoonists. He also found his footing in political matters. While he favors international subjects, his weekly output is often salted with civil liberties offerings, especially in the area of women's rights.

"I grew up in a time when it was just accepted that women would be housewives, and when we were sort of straddling the fence of the new morality. When I went to college, I was a little older than most, and had a decent perspective. And in the math department especially, you could see that women were just as efficient, just as good, just as bright as men. I became aware that they were having an even harder time getting jobs—it just seemed like a gross inequity." He agrees that most of today's good cartoonists share his views in favor of womens' lib, citing Ben Sargent, Doug Marlette, and the rest of the younger breed. "I don't think there are very many young people today who will side with Phyllis Schlafly or Anita Bryant."

Although he finds some civil liberties issues difficult cartoon fodder ("It was a tough topic when the ACLU supported the Klan"), Keefe enjoys most of the rights-oriented opportunities thrown at him. "The underlying issue is always very clear, a perfect setup for an editorial, when somebody's rights are being abridged—and not just at the expense of somebody else. These are prime situations for a cartoonist to illuminate."

With so much obvious love for his newly chosen profession, and with his enthusiastic interest in the topics of his drawings, we asked Mike Keefe whether any part of the cartoonist's life bothers him. He paused for a few moments, then observed, "Sometimes, I wonder what gives me the right to make these comments." But he goes on making them as he sees them.

'WOMEN PRIESTS! MY GOD, SINCE WHEN DO WOMEN PLAY A ROLE IN THE CHURCH?!'

... AND NOW THOSE IN FAVOR OF MY EMERGENCY POWERS RAISE YOUR HANDS!'

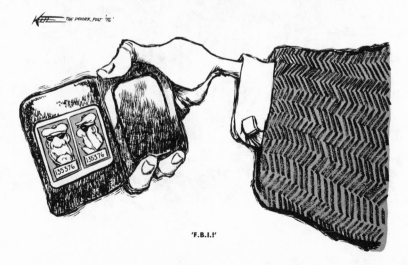

'F.B.I.!'

'FORGET THAT STUFF . . . THERE'S SOME REAL OBSCENITY NEXT DOOR!'

'HEY, I HAVEN'T FORGOTTEN YOU... BUT **SOMEONE** HAS TO SIT IN THE BACK!'

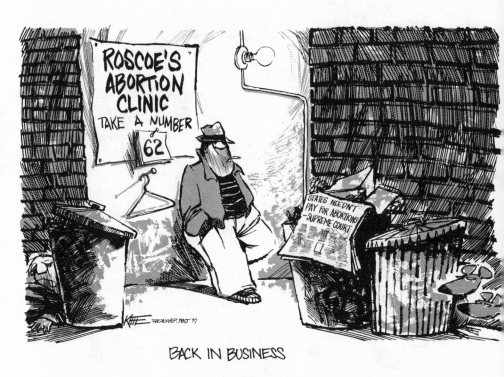

BACK IN BUSINESS

HITTING BETWEEN
THE EYES EVERY DAY

DON WRIGHT

"Impact is what makes a cartoon good and, in order to have impact, I'm not sure that you should be all that subtle. The best cartoons hit you squarely on the jaw, between the eyes. Magazines like *Newsweek* want cartoons that don't take too strong a position, that are funny. But cartoons should make a statement. And for that, I think we could do with a little less wit and a little more statement."

Those are strong words coming from someone who just had a cartoon featured in *Newsweek*. But Don Wright knows all about impact. In a 1974 *Time* article, the Pulitzer Prize–winning cartoonist was cited for being "hardest on Nixon"—and the title stuck. With inordinate modesty, Wright insists the reason that he liked drawing Nixon so much was that, being one who who has to "slave over caricatures," Nixon was "so easy to draw." "I miss him," he claims, "but I'm not willing to sacrifice the country just to have an easy subject around. Frankly," he adds, "I'm not sure we're out of danger yet. He may come back from the grave. I'm watching him very closely and, when I have the opportunity to comment on him, I do."

Wright is a newspaperman first and foremost. He started off in the business as a copyboy at the Miami *News,* then moved up to become a photographer. He considers himself "a damn good news photographer" and has the prizes to prove it. Wright's stint as a photographer was a very influential period in his life, changing him from a "reticent, unaggressive kid" into something quite different. As he sees it, "When you're forced into situations where you have to look at people who have been blown to bits, or cover fires, or be in the same room as John Kennedy, you're forced to react. It was a liberal education for me."

After five years as a photographer, Wright was promoted to picture editor at the *News*. For the two years that he was picture editor, he also did some writing, layout, and other general duties that broadened his creativity. His editor, Bill Baggs, upon noticing Wright's habit of summing up office situations in "nasty little cartoons" that would invariably find their way to the bulletin board, persuaded him to try his hand at editorial cartooning. After Wright walked out over a dispute with the managing editor, Baggs asked him to fill the vacancy left by their departing editorial cartoonist. "My initial reaction was that it was ridiculous," says Wright, "and I told him that I was just not interested in issues. But as I began to work at it and to read the wire more, I expanded my interests—I began to form opinions."

Wright's involvement with newspaper work doesn't end with drawing cartoons. He considers himself a devoted newspaperman and feels privileged to be part of the profession. "I work very hard at it—long, long hours. I'm totally involved in the operation of this newspaper. It's a challenge to keep it afloat."

Wright also feels that his civil libertarian tendencies have a lot to do with the environment in which he was raised. "I grew up in North Florida, playing with black kids. I couldn't help but realize that they lived in another area and weren't as well clothed; no matter how friendly they were they had to go off to their own world, which really wasn't much of a world. While it may sound trite, this first understanding of prejudice, inequality, and lack of opportunity stuck with me when I grew up. And these feelings just started coming out once I had the opportunity to express myself."

For one who has drawn some particularly biting cartoons on the subject of Anita Bryant's anti-homosexual crusade, Wright has a remarkably even-handed attitude toward the Miami community. "There will be people who disagree with me, but I think Miami is a fairly sophisticated community. It's almost totally unique. There are rednecks and almost every facet of people represented here. It affords me an opportunity to learn and develop as a person as well as to comment on an area that's growing rapidly and, in most cases, in the right direction."

Just as his community is changing, the issues Wright must deal with are continually evolving. Recently he has begun to concentrate on the First Amendment as it affects him as a newspaperman. "I'm dreadfully fearful of what's going on in the Burger court. I'm also a little leery of the reaction amongst newspapermen to this. We don't seem to be using the one weapon we have—the printed word—to apprise people, readers, of how much they stand to lose as individuals if we lose the battle to print and say what we want to say."

Wright won the Pulitzer Prize at about the time when the competition for it was just beginning to break loose, after being dominated for years by Mauldin and Herblock. During that time Oliphant—and a lot of fresh, young cartoonists with an Oliphantesque style—began appearing on the scene. Wright admits to picking up on Oliphant's style a bit too, but he also searched himself, tried new things, and eventually changed from a crayon technique to more line work. "I don't really feel that I have a style I'm satisfied with yet. It can still change, although it won't be based on other cartoonist's styles. It will be more me than anyone else. I have even begun to notice that some of the younger cartoonists have incorporated some of my nifty little tricks into their work."

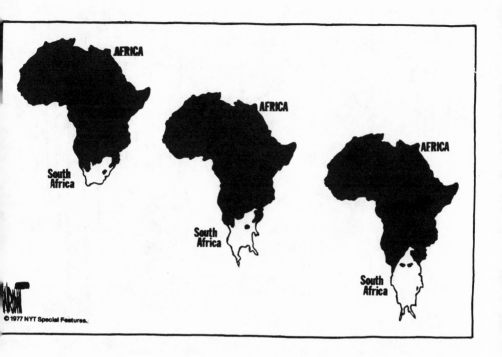

" 'ROOTS' IS CERTAINLY GETTING A LOT OF REACTION!"

"IF YOU DON'T DO ANYTHING ELSE WHEN YOU GROW UP, JUNIOR, JOIN THE NATIONAL RIFLE ASSOCIATION, PAY YOUR DUES AND FIGHT LIKE HELL AGAINST ALL THOSE LEFTWING SCREWBALLS PUSHING GUN CONTROLS."

I HAVE A BENT FOR SATIRE

PAUL SZEP

When Canadian-born cartoonist Paul Szep came to the Boston *Globe* in November of 1966, people in town didn't know what they were in for. "The *Globe* never had their own cartoonist," he says, "so a lot of the local politicians had never been done." In cartoons as in life, one person in particular stirred up the local blood. "There's this dastardly lady in town called Mrs. Hicks," Szep remembers, referring to the prominent opponent of school busing. "She's very fat. I got a lot of mail because of the way she was depicted visually. They had never seen a woman done like that." And Boston in the 1960s had an equal impact on Szep: "It really radicalized me. I grew up in a very conservative, apolitical town."

Szep was born and raised in Hamilton, Ontario, a large steel-producing town southwest of Toronto. He began drawing at an early age, landing a job in the sports pages of the Hamilton *Spectator* at the age of sixteen. "As a sports cartoonist I was influenced—as I guess everyone was—by Willard Mullin, the great American sports cartoonist." While he had "no interest" in politics at that time, he "always wanted to do political cartoons because it seemed like a natural outlet for caricature." Caricature and satire are Szep's first loves, as the portly Mrs. Hicks would eventually find out.

Szep worked in the local steel mills while he attended the Ontario College of Art, majoring in illustration. After graduation in 1964, he decided to try his luck at syndicating his own comic strip, "Oh Hungry." "I really had a super setup. I would work on the strip in the morning and play golf in the afternoon. A wonderful life." The bubble burst, however, when the strip didn't sell, so Szep headed for Toronto and a job as an illustrator, graphic designer, and cartoonist for the *Financial Post*.

While at the *Post,* "I sent my stuff down to a fellow named Bill Sanders on the Kansas City *Star.* He was president of the Association of Editorial Cartoonists, and I just asked him if he knew of any jobs. I was very naive." But Sanders was related to Gene Graham, a journalism professor and cartoonist, who also happened to direct the Boston *Globe*'s summer intern program. The paper had been looking for its own cartoonist for three or four years. They invited Szep down for a two-week tryout in June of 1966 and gave him the job in November. The move was momentous. "The big issue was Vietnam," he recalls, "and I was sold" on it. But "from the moment I came down here, I realized there was another side. That was really a great breakthrough for me. As a Canadian I used to see the American government as the knight on the white charger. I suddenly realized that they fucked up on Vietnam—something as *big* as Vietnam. The best and the brightest were really not the best and the brightest." His antiwar cartoons date from early 1967.

Even though his own sensibility was in the process of radical transformation, Szep says that commenting on the American political scene posed no serious problem. "One of the two things I could do was caricature, and I think I had a bent for satire. I just took the issues as they came along."

A Szep cartoon is dominated by a strong line, and more often than not by powerful—even melodramatic—faces. Greatly influenced by David Low, he eschews the type of visual joke that dominates the profession today, attributing its prominence to television. "To maintain an audience, the cartoon has to be entertaining in itself because you're competing against the old tube. People see things on the six o'clock news; they saw the war at six o'clock. To hit them over the head every day, or to go for the jugular every day, like you could have done at one time, just doesn't work. The problem is that you can carry it across the line to where it's no longer an editorial cartoon. I've come to realize that you need humor and ridicule, but you have to make an editorial statement."

Szep cartoons have no problem in doing precisely that. Civil liberties are particularly important to him because they alone "differentiate this society from an Eastern European society. For the worker who is not conscious politically, and isn't in the position to express his thoughts, they make the difference." Yet, at one time, Szep wanted to modify the Constitution in order to provide for more public policy referendums. No more. "If people did make changes today, the first thing they would go after would be freedom of the press. They would close out investigative reporting, the guts of the whole business. That sort of mentality is very dangerous and it's pervasive."

Szep's love of caricature and "bent for satire" have brought him two Pulitzer Prizes in the last four years—perhaps an unprecedented feat—and an honorary doctorate from Framingham State. His cartoons are syndicated internationally by

McNaught and are collected in three volumes; the most recent
—*Them Damned Pitchers*—is just out. But he has no plans
for resting, particularly when the country is in the throes of
what he sees as a "false conservatism."

"I look at issues like the abortion bill being debated here,"
he says, commenting on legislation to withhold state Medicaid
funds for abortions, "and I can see that it's a bill directed
against poor people. A rich person won't be affected. That
mentality I find frightening."

"ACCURSED BE HE THAT FIRST INVENTED WAR."

"Go forth and infiltrate!"

"HEAR NO EVIL . . . SPEAK NO EVIL . . . SEE NO EVIL."

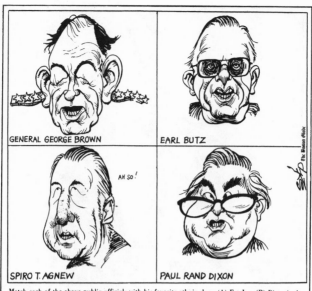

Match each of the above public officials with his favorite ethnic slurs: (A) Fat Jap; (B) Dirty Arab; (C) Jew Power; (D) Loose-shoed Blacks

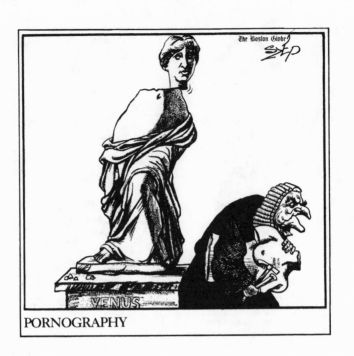

PORNOGRAPHY

"I agree, it's really outrageous . . . it's only 38 percent"

"NO, I DIDN'T INVITE HIM. . . . I THOUGHT YOU DID"

NEWS ITEM: Justice Department to investigate FBI agents in new disclousures of burglaries

RHODESIAN UPRISING

A MINDSET
OF ABSOLUTE IRREVERENCE

BEN SARGENT

Ben Sargent is a soft-spoken, young cartoonist who delights in drawing on civil liberties themes—a consistent advocate who sees himself as an "editorialist with a mindset of absolute irreverence for everything." Well, perhaps not everything. Sargent's cartoons convey a deep commitment to individual freedom. Drawn in a style which sets his work apart from many of the more mainstream cartoonists today, Sargent's cartoons are like an encyclopedia of current civil liberties issues, everything from abortion and deprogramming to plea bargaining and Fourth Amendment search and seizure violations.

"I try to depict civil liberties principles as vividly as I can," says Sargent, "because people seem to have a fundamental ignorance about them, especially here in Texas where there's a strong 'lock 'em up and throw away the key' mentality toward law and order. That attitude is a real danger here—especially with our state legislature."

Sargent came to editorial cartooning by a circuitous route. Born in Amarillo in West Texas, where both his parents worked for the Amarillo *News & Globe Times,* a daily paper with a circulation of 85,000, Sargent always conceived of himself as a newspaperman. At age fourteen he began his career as a copyboy and later became a proofreader and reporter in Amarillo. After receiving a journalism degree from the University of Texas in 1970, Sargent went to work as a reporter for the Corpus Christi *Caller-Times,* graduating from there to covering the state capital in Austin for UPI and Long News Service (an independent, state capital news service in Texas), and, ultimately, as a capital reporter for the *American-Statesman.*

Through all this, the thirty-year-old Sargent remained an inveterate doodler. After a while, his drawings made during long-winded sessions of the legislature came more and more to resemble satiric cartoons, and they came to the attention of the editorial page editor at Sargent's paper. "I was a fairly mediocre reporter," Sargent recalls, "just writing day-to-day, bread and butter stuff. I never even thought about doing editorial cartoons because cartoonists are so few and far between here. I don't think there are more than six or seven cartoonists

in the whole state of Texas. But the editor here saw my drawings, and he asked me to do illustrations for the paper part-
time. Then I started doing cartoons three days a week until
now I draw one every day. I'm the first full-time cartoonist
the *American-Statesman* has ever employed."

Sargent attributes his editorial point-of-view to his parents
influence and growing up liberal in West Texas. "My parents
were 'the liberals' in Amarillo," he recalls. "Amarillo is still
kind of a cow town, wide-open, crazy and receptive to ideas.
It's sort of a hot-bed of right-wing activity, and I found it a
challenge to be a liberal there. Austin, where almost everyone is
liberal, is almost too comfortable for me. I really respect those
few liberals scattered across Texas, in places like Houston,
Odessa, and Amarillo, who are really challenged because of
their ideas."

Sargent is fortunate to work for a newspaper which supports
his outlook—"we're just about the only paper here opposed
to the death penalty," he says—and he finds that his years as
a reporter and rewrite man come in handy in depicting local
affairs. State politics, especially, remains a passion. "I do at
least two cartoons a week on Texas politics because it's so
incredible," says Sargent. "Texas politicians go to all sorts of
strange excesses of fatuousness and stupidity. It has sort of a
special quality all its own."

Perhaps because of this environment, Sargent's cartoons
have a special quality all their own as well. It is a strong civil
libertarian diet that tends to stick in the craw of most Texans.
And it's been drawn by a person who says with a sense of
self-satisfaction, "Now I'm getting paid for what I used to get
in trouble for when I was in school—drawing in class."

FELLOW TEXANS, PROPOSITION Nº 3 WILL ALLOW YOUR CRIMINAL JUSTICE SYSTEM TO DENY BAIL TO CRIMINALS ACCUSED OF COMMITTING CRIMES WHILE FREE ON BAIL.

IT'S SOMETHING WE NEED IF WE'RE GOING TO SWEEP CRIME FROM OUR STREETS. SAY WE HAD A DOPE-CRAZED KILLER... WHAM! WE COULD LOCK 'IM UP!

A DEPRAVED PUSHER... BAM! WE PUT 'IM AWAY! A SNEAKING BURGLAR... BOOM! INTO TH' SLAMMER!!

AND DON'T GIMME NO NAMBY-PAMBY, RIGHTS-OF-THE-ACCUSED, SOB-SISTER STUFF ABOUT "INNOCENT UNTIL PROVEN GUILTY," EITHER!

A CRIMINAL IS A CRIMINAL, WHETHER HE'S GUILTY OR INNOCENT!!

BEN SARGENT...

LANDMARKS IN TEXAS JUSTICE ☆ ☆ ☆

TERRY DENSON & STEPHEN ORLANDO
OFFENSE: Causing the drowning of an unruly Mexican-American prisoner.
PUNISHMENT: One year probation.

FRANK HAYES
OFFENSE: Shooting to death an unruly Mexican-American prisoner.
PUNISHMENT: 2 to 10 years' imprisonment.

JOE TORRES & RICHARD MORALES
OFFENSE: Being unruly Mexican-American prisoners.
PUNISHMENT: DEATH.

BEN SARGENT~
©'77 The Austin American-Statesman

THINGS WERE
MUCH WORSE
THAN I EVER EXPECTED

DOUG MARLETTE

Doug Marlette of the Charlotte *Observer* may not be the youngest editorial cartoonist working for a daily paper in America, but he certainly looks the part. "My age and appearance startle people," he says. "People who only know me through my work expect me to be older, shorter, with a darker complexion and bearded. I guess it's something in the way I draw."

Instead, the twenty-eight-year-old Marlette is tall, blond and baby-faced. But, as his readers know full well, beneath that innocent-seeming veneer lies a talent that delights in depicting current topics—especially civil liberties issues—with such a biting wit that within one month of Marlette's arrival at the *Observer* in 1972, petitions were being circulated among readers urging that Marlette be reassigned to an unemployment line. And the hate mail has kept pouring in daily.

Yet Marlette is no radical interloper imported from other climes by the management of the *Observer* to offend the sensibilities of the Old South. Rather, he is a product of that tradition—born in Greensboro, North Carolina, and raised in Laurel, Mississippi, which, while Marlette was growing up there, was known nationally as the "Home of the White Knights of the Ku Klux Klan."

"I've always thought of myself and my ideas as very much a product of the South," says Marlette. "I went to the Magnolia Street Baptist Church in Laurel, Mississippi, and they taught me about the Sermon on the Mount. In my high school civics class, they taught me about the Constitution and the Bill of Rights. I guess I just always thought they were serious about it."

Because Marlette took what he was taught seriously, he applied to his local draft board for conscientious objector status while a student at Florida State University in Tallahassee. His father, a corpsman in the Marines, had been transferred to Sanford, Florida, in the central part of the state, where local boards took a dim view of such applications.

"My family wasn't thrilled about my applying for a CO," Marlette recalls. "I didn't get a lot of encouragement from my community either. By this time, though, I had been doing cartoons for my college paper for several years. I submitted a portfolio of my antiwar cartoons to the board to demonstrate that my feelings about warfare were 'the product of long-held beliefs expressed publicly prior to applying for CO classification.' And my CO was granted."

After looking unsuccessfully for six months for appropriate alternative service—"you know," Marlette says, "emptying bed pans or being a forest ranger"—Marlette was hired by the College Press Service (CPS), a national syndicate for college newspapers which fulfilled the Selective Service System's requirements as a nonprofit organization whose work was in the national interest. Ironically, most of Marlette's work for CPS consisted of antiwar cartoons.

While the student and antiwar movements have long since become a part of Marlette's past, the imprint of those times are still an important element in his creative processes. As Reese Cleghorn, former editorial page editor of the *Observer*, recently noted: "Some of Marlette's best work comes just after we have had a meaningful exchange about a proposed cartoon. On those occasions, he lapses into suffering and links himself to some of the great cartoonist sufferers of history. Honoré Daumier, he will tell me dolefully, was imprisoned by King Louis Philippe, and Art Young was brought to trial for sedition by the Wilson administration. I remind him that we are merely discussing the merits of a cartoon and that he faces neither the slammer nor a charge of treason. But I do not go too far . . . The worst thing you can do to a cartoonist is deprive him of his suffering."

Marlette himself doesn't see his point of view growing out of some intangible anguish, but merely from what he sees around himself every day. "When I was in college," he says, "everyone counseled me to 'wait until I got into the real world, and then I'd find out what life was really all about and straighten up.' They were right about a heavy dose of reality being an eye-opener. I found out that things were much worse than I ever expected."

That view is expressed in Marlette's cartoons through a remarkably staunch and consistent civil libertarian stance. His cartoons rarely, if ever, seem ambiguous. Instead, one finds strong, cleverly thought out statements on issues like affirmative action, pornography, capital punishment, amnesty, women's rights, and court-ordered busing.

The busing controversy is particularly illustrative, both of Marlette's development and his surprising regional chauvinism. "Charlotte was one of the first cities in the country to experience court-ordered busing," he recalls. "And it's worked here, but it hasn't been easy—it's been a struggle. Being here during that period was a valuable learning experience for me, and indicative too of how the South has changed. It has been more difficult for people in the South to develop a commitment to civil liberties, I think, than for people in the rest of the nation. But once people here develop beliefs like a commitment to integration, they're strongly forged. And I trust people like that."

Change has not led Marlette to complacency, however. His work is targeted at, to quote editor Cleghorn's alliterative Southern prose, "the hortatory emissions—the flapdoodle, piffle, and pettifoggery—of those leaders who have mistaken their molehills for Olympus."

"YOU'RE DISGUSTING!"

"WELL, ACTUALLY THERE IS **ONE** DOOR YOU COULD OPEN FOR ME!"

"SO THERE I WAS....TRYING TO DECIDE WHAT TO DO ABOUT THE TROUBLESOME PROBLEM OF HUMAN RIGHTS WHEN SUDDENLY IT CAME TO ME—BOOM! NO HUMANS, NO HUMAN RIGHTS!"

"IT'S MY FAVORITE COLOR!"

" AND JUST WHERE DO YOU THINK YOU'RE GOING?...."

"WHAT'S A NICE GIRL LIKE YOU DOING IN A PLACE LIKE THAT?"

"REACTION TO YOUR WIRETAPPING APOLOGY SOUNDS GOOD, CHIEF!"

"NO, I DIDN'T DEMAND TO TALK TO THE PRESIDENT—I DEMANDED A MILLION DOLLARS, A PEPPERONI PIZZA AND AN END TO OPPRESSION OF LEFT-HANDED PEOPLES—YOU MUST WANT THE TERRORISTS TWO FLIGHTS UP!"

"HOLD IT RIGHT THERE!...OH, SORRY, MISS—WE THOUGHT YOU WERE ADMINISTER THE SACRAMENTS!..."

I DON'T LIKE TO SEE UNCOMMON MEN SUPPRESSED

BILL MAULDIN

In his autobiography, *The Brass Ring,* Bill Mauldin reveals that his critical attitude toward mandates and regulations began early. His high school in Phoenix, Arizona, "was as modern in its outlook as any public high school of its time," he writes, "but you could still find things to criticize if you were so inclined. I was. When I decided a rule was chickenshit, I found a way to defy it in print."

The tendency to oppose the established order has gotten Mauldin into lots of scrapes in the forty years since he left Phoenix Union High. But it has also served him—and his millions of readers since World War II—quite well. Fifty-seven years of age may seem a mite young to be one of the grand-daddies of today's political cartoonists, but his constant battle against "chickenshit rules" earns Bill Mauldin that status.

His New Mexico childhood was a prime factor in the creation of his independent status. "My parents were too busy having domestic upheavals to direct us in everything we did, and they were always broke," recalls Mauldin. "They split up when I was fourteen, and that's when I left home. And though this is one of those things that's supposed to create chronic convicts, they gave me a strong sense of being loved. I never felt they would let me sink if they could possibly save me."

Mauldin kept himself from sinking, acting the gadfly in high school, and eventually—after a year studying art in Chicago —landed in the army just prior to the outbreak of World War II. While he saw action as a soldier in the Sicilian corridor, most of his time was spent behind a drawing board. This produced some of the most incisive—and black humorous—views of war and soldiering to flow from an artist's pen. His Willie and Joe cartoons for *Stars & Stripes* were wry depictions of the war-is-hell life of the average infantryman and won him his first Pultizer Prize at the ripe age of twenty-three.

He drew scruffy-bearded, sloppily dressed fighters because, he says, "I knew these guys best, and it gave the typical soldier an outlet for his frustrations, a chance to blow off steam." It also got Mauldin into hot water with the brass more than once. General George S. Patton, whose regal manner, ivory-handled six-shooters, and medieval view of the enlisted man-officer relationship Mauldin satired, tried to push the cartoonist into more supportive activities. "I don't know where you got those stripes on your arm," Patton told Mauldin, "but you'd put 'em to a lot better use teaching respect to soldiers instead of encouraging them to bitch and beef and gripe and run around with beards on their faces." The feisty artist was not swayed, and his biting commentaries on officers' privileges, ill-equipped foxhole dwellers, and arrest-happy MPs continued throughout the duration of the war.

Mauldin continues, "I think my cartoons created a certain amount of introspection in the army. The army, of course, overreacted. What I was trying to say was that the idea of the enlisted man as peasant and the officer as gentleman may have made some sense way back when that was the way it was, but it wasn't that way any longer."

Despite his reputation, however, Mauldin bridles at the familiar appelation "spokesman for the little guy."

"I never thought of the people I drew as 'little guys,' " he says. "I was supposed to be the champion of the enlisted man, the common man. Well, I don't really have much use for the common man y' know? Never did. I just don't like to see uncommon men suppressed. And in the ranks of common men are a lot of splendid characters who should be allowed to shine."

For a time after the war, it looked as if Bill Mauldin would fade from the scene. By the early fifties, many viewed the civilian Mauldin as a has-been, a war-weary anachronism. The cartoonist tried his hand at a few different careers: He acted in two movies (including *The Red Badge of Courage*) and even ran for Congress, losing as a Democrat in a heavily Republican upstate New York district. In 1958 he landed at the St. Louis *Post-Dispatch* and finally hit his postwar stride. Some of the best pro-civil rights cartoons of the late fifties and early sixties were inked by Bill Mauldin, irking Southern politicians the way his bedraggled fighters had bothered Patton.

The sentiments in his civil rights cartoons sprang from the same early anti-authoritarianism that motivated his wartime work. "I think all attitudes are formed as a reaction to growing up. It's fair to say my civil-liberties consciousness is a result of that. It seemed to me I was always being told, or seeing other people told, that you must accept limits for one reason or another. I saw Mexican kids being told that they couldn't hope to achieve certain things. I was told that, because my parents had no money, I couldn't go to college; I couldn't do this, I couldn't do that.

"In other words, you were told that you had to have limited expectations. Well, I never bought that."

His stance on racial prejudice—so clearly defined that his cartoons on the subject won him a second Pulitzer in 1958—is also "reactive," as he puts it.

"I was always very conscious of prejudice. Take anti-Semitism, for example, which was absolutely endemic to the Southwest—yet there were practically no Jews there when I was growing up. I don't recall as a little kid ever knowing a Jew, but you heard jokes about 'em all the time. And there were very few blacks in New Mexico, yet you always heard jokes about coons, and jigs, and burrheads and so on, told by people who had never even seen a black! That's the point—this prejudice was unjust from the beginning, because the people who practiced it didn't know what the hell they were talking about."

His southwestern boyhood also gave him a special perspective on another hot civil liberties topic, gun control, although the judgments he draws are different from the standard Eastern brand.

"I'm not exactly a pro-gun nut," he says, "but I think there are as many kooks on the anti-gun side as the pro-gun side—maybe even more. So I've always been, in a sense, the devil's advocate, balancing out someone like Herblock. Herb has always been strongly anti-gun. My feeling is that I don't want to live in a society where only crooks and cops are armed."

As a founding father of modern political cartooning, Mauldin likes to pay particular attention to the state of the art, of which he is more than critical. Too many of the younger cartoonists are success-conscious, believes Mauldin, because of the "baleful influence" of *Time* magazine's "star system." The result: "They all want to imitate Ronald Searle, and they're not as effective or as deadly as they can be. They're a little too damn responsible."

Mauldin has a critical word for much of what he sees and hears—a necessity for one who has remained a successful cartoonist as long as he has. Yet he manages to be quite good natured, punctuating his salty language with a lot of laugher. He turns dark only when he speaks of the current conservative trend in the country and his fears of the coming right-wing backlash. "I think civil liberties are in a lot of trouble, I really do," he says. "But political cartooning is gonna be one of those areas where it'll be hard to put 'em down."

It has *always* been hard to put Bill Mauldin down, and the artist himself states the reason as succinctly as anyone can: "I'm against oppression. By whomever."

"Th' hell with it, sir. Let's go back to the front."

"I tried one of them labor-management argyments wit' Looten-ant Atkins."

"Mommy says I gotta quit seein' ya, Butch. Ya got minorities or somethin'."

"Of course, you mustn't misunderstand us — we all want a free press!"

"I TRUST YOU'LL ONLY BE USING THIS STUFF IN THE INTEREST OF NATIONAL SECURITY, MISTER..."

"BUDDY, IF THAT GUN AIN'T REGISTERED, YOU'RE IN WORSE TROUBLE THAN I AM."

"THE CONVEYOR BELT WAS A GREAT IDEA."

"...MAKES YOU WONDER HOW THEY EVER MANAGED TO KILL BUFFALO."

"Hm-m....I see you need a small dose of civil rights."

"You can't fly on one wing."

"May we have a statement on Human Rights in New Hampshire?"

"What's it like to live with a second-class citizen?"

A place for everything and everything in its place.

A GOOD CARTOONIST
IS LIKE A LOADED GUN

MIKE PETERS

"Cartooning is not a fair art," says Mike Peters of the Dayton *Daily News* in Dayton, Ohio. "You can never treat anyone justly. Most cartoonists like me—who like to attack—are like loaded guns. Every morning we start looking through the newspaper for a target to blast. That's our function."

Peters has been firing his weapon around Dayton and the nation for the past nine years with mixed results. On the positive side, Peters' newspaper *has* been picketed twice because of one of his cartoons, events which bring a note of pride to Peters' voice in recounting them. But lately, the hate mail and the threatening phone calls, at least from the Dayton area, have been tapering off. Apparently Peters' local audience has accustomed itself to his barbs, and now the only hostile voices to brighten his day come from faraway readers who have encountered one of his cartoons placed through syndication.

"I picture my job as very similar to the little kid who says that the emperor has no clothes," says Peters. "When I started cartooning—my first cartoon for the Dayton *Daily News* appeared on Nixon's inauguration day in 1969—I decided that since a cartoon is an inherently unfair medium and you've got this ability to attack, I'd do just that: attack and be one-sided. I mean, the dream of every editorial cartoonist is to get picketed. It's got to be."

One would hardly guess from Peters' self-styled job description that he still thinks of himself, at age thirty-four, as a happy-go-lucky kid from St. Louis. But, in fact, he sees himself as a "world-is-my-oyster" individual, living the schizophrenic life of an enfant terrible at work and an average, middle-class American existence at home. Perhaps it's what Peters calls his "weird growing-up time" which accounts for his dual existence.

Peters' mother was the host of an afternoon TV show in St. Louis for twenty-two years—*The Charlotte Peters Show,* a talk and variety hour that was on the air from noon to 1:00 P.M. While he was growing up, Peters made frequent appearances on the show, drawing pictures for the audience or dancing with his mother. St. Louis and environs knew him as "Little Mike." "I was always on the show," he recalls, "and it was fun growing up in that environment because everybody knew mom and me through mom."

One of the people who knew "Little Mike" because of his mother was Pulitzer Prize–winning cartoonist Bill Mauldin, then with the St. Louis *Post-Dispatch*. It was through Mauldin that Peters' interest in cartooning was kindled, and that interest became a passion after Peters saw Mauldin's face on the cover of *Time* magazine in 1958 when the cartoonist won his second Pulitzer. "When I saw it," recalls Peters, "I said to myself, 'my God! that's it for me . . . that's what I want to be; I mean if a cartoonist can get his picture on the cover of *Time*, what more is there?' I saw a chance to do something and still have a good time for the rest of my life—being able to draw, get pissed at people, and mouth off whenever you want to. There's nothing better than that."

When Peters graduated from Washington University in St. Louis in the mid-sixties with a B.F.A., he went to Chicago to see his mentor Mauldin and showed him his cartoons for the first time. Mauldin helped him to get a job with the art staff of the Chicago *Daily News*. Within a year, with the help of Chicago *Daily News* cartoonist John Fischetti, Peters was offered a job drawing editorial cartoons for the op ed page, but just as he was about to start his new endeavor, he received a letter from the Selective Service System which began, "Greetings . . ." A life-long ambition realized quickly turned into basic training at Fort Leonard Wood, Missouri.

Peters did not let a little thing like the Vietnam war stand in the way of his ambitions. Shortly after induction, he began drawing cartoons for the base newspaper at Fort Leonard Wood, was kept there after basic, and ultimately spent the bulk of his two years of military service as a cartoonist for a base newspaper in Okinawa. Peters looks back on his situation in the military as a vignette out of "M*A*S*H"—lounging on Okinawa watching the B–52s come and go. For someone who had developed a deep commitment to the civil rights and antiwar movements in college in the sixties, it was an absurd situation.

The experience kindled a sense of outrage in Peters that found its expression in his work after he finished his military service. Following a short stint at the Chicago *Daily News*, Peters was hired for his present position, again through the help of Bill Mauldin. "Mauldin called up the editor here and told him about me," Peters recalls, "and the editor said, 'Fine, I'll hire him right now without even seeing his cartoons.' "

Peters was fortunate in finding a liberal paper that encouraged him to sharpen his wit along with his pencils. Richard Nixon was a favorite target, along with a whole spectrum of civil liberties issues, especially Watergate, women's rights, and the myriad abuses of the FBI and CIA. In 1976, Peters published a book of his cartoons on the demise and fall of Nixon titled *The Nixon Chronicles*.

Today, Peters has achieved his life's goal of having fun by speaking his mind and getting paid for it. Through United Features, his work is syndicated in 170 newspapers, although Peters finds it puzzling that "odd papers pick me up; it must be the water I drink." In addition, his cartoons often appear in publications like *The New Republic,* which recently featured one of his drawings on its cover.

Peters' editorial point of view is one of the most acerbic on the market. "I wish there were more ways for people to speak their mind and get paid for it," he says. "And I wish that people who write editorials would stop being so goddamn 'fair.' As long as you're being 'fair,' whatever you're putting across is going to be watered down."

I CAN'T TAKE IT ANYMORE... THE BURGLARIES... THE BREAK-INS... RUNNING FROM THE COPS... HIDING OUT IN FLEA-RIDDEN MOTELS... CHARLIE, YOU'VE GOT TO QUIT THE FBI.

WE'VE GOT TO DEPROGRAM JUNIOR—HE'S RUN OFF AND JOINED THE PRESBYTERIANS...

THE CONSTITUTION IS A
HELL OF A DOCUMENT

PAUL CONRAD

"I think we've been laughing at these issues long enough. We've got too many problems. We don't have that much time for laughter anymore."

Paul Conrad needn't worry—the right people never laugh at his cartoons. Richard Nixon didn't; he put Conrad on his Enemies List. Former Los Angeles mayor Sam Yorty didn't; he sued Conrad for $6 million. Fred Hartley didn't; the Union Oil Company chairman recently lost his $4 million libel suit against the cartoonist.

Chances are, in fact, that very few people laugh heartily at Paul Conrad's work. The cartoons over his familiar heavy black-ink signature, running for the last sixteen years on the editorial pages of the Los Angeles *Times,* are biting, incisive, and to the point, but generally not funny. Telling him that doesn't offend him. "I love the use of humor, satire, all the rest of it," he says. "But I'm not sure all that is possible today, with the urgency of the matters this nation faces."

This sense of urgency is easily identified in Conrad's cartoons. No Oliphantish puns, no Feifferian subtlety. To Paul Conrad, gray is a shade to be used in drawing; his ideas are in black and white. And, although he's received more than his share of criticism, lawsuits, and obscene telephone calls, he insists, "I'll continue to draw cartoons just as I have been, because I think there are a great many injustices that have to be taken care of."

Conrad attends to those injustices by vilifying the ones he considers opponents of civil rights. For example, Mayor Yorty's suit was motivated by a cartoon that graphically called into question his mental state. In 1968, when the reactionary mayor was publicly bucking for the position of secretary of defense in President-elect Nixon's cabinet, Conrad penned a drawing showing four men in white, barely hiding a straitjacket, with Yorty saying into the phone, "I've got to go now. I've been appointed Secretary of Defense, and the Secret Service men are here." Conrad's position on the Enemies List was secured by similarly unsubtle skewerings. That one piece of notorious recognition has caused him more concern than any of his other awards—which include a pair of Pulitzers.

"Quite frankly, at first I was delighted to be on the Enemies List. Our national editor, Ed Guthman (now at the Philadelphia *Inquirer*), was on the first one, and he just hung that over my head: 'How effective do you think you are, if you didn't even make the list?' Well, there came the second list, and, boy, did I show Ed!"

He continues, barely disguising the annoyance in his voice: "But you start to think about it, and you do a slow burn when you realize that this was going on in *our* White House. I think it was an unpardonable offense, that any administration would stoop to such a level. I'll never understand Nixon's kind of mentality."

Nor, for that matter, will Paul Conrad ever neglect it in his work. Unlike many editorial writers and cartoonists who were willing to leave the former president alone subsequent to his resignation, Conrad continues to aim an occasional barb. "A lot of people would really like to forget Nixon," he says, "but I absolutely refuse to!"

It is not only the individual enemies of civil rights who feel the wrath of Paul Conrad's pen. Organized groups and movements, in government, business, or the private sector, are not spared the vitriol. The CIA and its illegal domestic spying, the Supreme Court and its perceived stand against the press, and the growing anti-gay rights movement are frequent targets of Conrad attacks.

The strident liberalism he displays in his cartoons would seem to belie his upbringing. Born fifty-four years ago, Conrad was raised in a rock-ribbed Republican family in Cedar Rapids, Iowa, and later moved to Des Moines. He attended Catholic parochial schools and didn't become serious about drawing until he was midway through the University of Iowa.

"I was working my way through college on the GI Bill and by playing string bass in a dance band. We had a swinging outfit—vibes, clarinet, drums, bass, and piano," he remembers.

"With two years to go, I was majoring in art and didn't know what I wanted to do. I had seen too much of the musician's life and knew I didn't want to do *that*. Well, I ran into a friend from Des Moines, who was editor of the school paper. He suggested I try a few cartoons. I did one the next morning, and I've been doing them ever since."

Although his thirteen years in Denver (at the *Post*) and sixteen in Los Angeles have seen him move more strongly in the area of rights, Conrad remains an enigma—and an infuriating one at that—to many civil libertarians. Despite his solid support for women's rights, Conrad is an ardent pro-lifer, and some of his anti-abortion cartoons are jarring, to say the least. He feels no need to justify his position, seeing it as perfectly consistent with his viewpoint on other matters of liberty: "Look, I just don't know where life begins, but I know it begins somewhere. I hate to think we're at that point in our civilization where human life is held at such a low degree. It seems to me that the civil libertarians would be on the side of the unborn baby."

He's been over this ground before, but his sense of conviction makes it seem like the first time he's put forth the argument. His disgust over the matter is not displayed toward people who favor abortion rights; rather, he reserves his anger for those he deems so close-minded they can't see the other side.

"A woman on the ACLU staff out here told me that my name came up for an award they give, but I was turned down because a few of them said, 'No way, because of his stand on abortion.' That seemed a wee small on the part of the Union."

He gives a sigh. "If that's the case, what good are all the damn awards anyway?"

Criticism fazes Paul Conrad but briefly, if at all, and his moment of reflection is soon over. There are more problems to draw, and more people to stop laughing.

"The Constitution is a hell of a document, if we would just give it a whirl," he says. "But too many people would like to dismantle it as a convenience.

"Well, I'll have no part of *that!*"

SENATE BANS 'SATURDAY NIGHT SPECIAL' — NEWS ITEM

"...COPY BOY...!"

"YOU'D BETTER LOOK AT WHAT I'VE GOT ON HIM!"

THE MEN WHO PLAYED GOD

"I HAVE THE RIGHT TO REMAIN SILENT..."

'WOMB TO TOMB'

IF YOU ARE IN FAVOR OF CAPITAL PUNISHMENT, PUSH THIS BUTTON

"THANKSGIVING...THAT'S WHEN YOU GET THE TURKEY AND I GET THE FEATHERS!"

I LOVE A CHARADE

THE CIA'S LITERARY CRITIC

CONFRONTING PEOPLE WITH WHAT THEY DON'T WANT TO SEE

TONY AUTH

"**P**art of the job as a cartoonist," says Tony Auth, "is to confront people with things they really don't want to see." Auth currently jars people's senses daily in the pages of the Philadelphia *Inquirer*, and his work is distributed nationally by the Washington *Post* Writers' Group.

His cartoons weren't always so widely disseminated, however. In 1971, after looking for work on a daily paper for five years, Auth had accumulated hundreds of rejection letters. One paper in Hawaii wrote him pointedly, "When you grow up and mature, there may be room for you in American journalism." Five years later, he won the Pulitzer Prize for editorial cartooning.

How Auth went from pariah to prize-winner says a lot about what our nation has gone through in the past decade. Auth was a student at U.C.L.A., drawing cartoons for the Daily *Bruin* and planning for a career as a medical illustrator, when the first battalion of U.S. Marines landed in Vietnam. "Vietnam got me turned on," Auth recalls. "I'd done cartoons for the *Bruin* all through college, but it wasn't political, just campus happenings. *Open City*, a weekly trying to compete with the Los Angeles *Free Press*, asked me if I'd like to draw a weekly political cartoon for them. I said, 'O.K., I'll try'—I didn't know if I could do it. About a year later, I discovered that not only could I do it, but I loved doing it."

Auth went to see Paul Conrad, the Los Angeles *Times'* editorial cartoonist, to ask him how to go about getting a job on a daily paper. "He told me that my work wasn't bad," says Auth, "but that drawing once a week wasn't enough because you never get into stride. The real test is drawing day after day." Taking Conrad's advice to heart, Auth contacted his alma mater, the *Bruin*, and drew three cartoons a week for them for the next four years. He also began syndicating his work through the underground Sawyer Press Syndicate.

Auth found his stride, but despite hundreds of applications, no daily paper he could call his own. "I was on the verge of frustration at that point," he recalls. "I had been trying to get into this field professionally for four years. It's a tiny field and there aren't many openings. Most papers don't have the guts to hire someone, anyway. They'd rather subscribe to four or five cartoonists and be able to take their pick without hassling with someone who has a strong mind or will."

Then in 1971, Auth was told that the Philadelphia *Inquirer,* which had just been sold by Walter Annenberg to the Knight-Ridder chair, was looking for a cartoonist. "I really lucked out," says Auth. "Creed Black, the editor then, decided that the best thing the *Inquirer* could do would be to search for a young, unknown cartoonist rather than hire somebody with a big name." After several months of searching, they hired Auth.

Auth's drawing style is considered unique by many critics of the art. While Auth himself sees various influences on his work —Pat Oliphant, Ronald Searle, James Thurber—his drawings exude a flair that is pure Auth. "After a year at the *Inquirer,*" he says, "I was very unhappy with my drawings. I liked my rough sketches, which are done without any conscious effort in about ten seconds, more than the finished art. So I started using a light box to trace my rough drawings, and I've been much happier with my work."

The views expressed in Auth's cartoons, especially in his civil liberties cartoons, often emanate from an unconscious, gut sense of things as well. "I'm very concerned about abuse of power," he says, "but I'm more concerned about the institutional abuse of power because that's something that we, as a society, are really much better equipped to deal with, and it's also something that we're more tolerant of. When I draw a civil liberties cartoon, I almost always deal with the institutions rather than the personalities. Of course I have drawn Presidents quite often. But in my work I really want to be sure that the blame gets placed where it belongs. It's just too easy to blame everything on the President."

Living and working in Philadelphia, where Mayor Frank Rizzo has created a civil liberties disaster area, Auth finds himself frequently drawing local cartoons with civil liberties themes. "The mayor is a funny guy," he says. "He loves Philadelphia, but he's also a cop and his loyalties reflect his many years on the police force. I did one cartoon recently, after an *Inquirer* investigative series showed that the police here regularly use intimidation and force to get confessions from suspects and witnesses. Rizzo tolerates that kind of behavior by the police—and even encourages it—because that's the way the police force was when he came through it. Rizzo gets carried away with his power sometimes. In 1972, when President Nixon came here to sign the Revenue-Sharing

Bill, he had virtually every peaceful picketer at Independence Hall arrested in spite of a court injunction—it was incredible."

While a confrontation with the world of Tony Auth may not be the most comfortable view of the current state of our freedoms, it is a perspective that grew up in a decade of turmoil that refuses to become complacent.

'The charge against you, Mr. Schorr, is assault with intent to commit truth.'

'Don't worry. When I kiss him, he'll turn into
a great attorney general.'

'Of course my hair transplants will be covered by sick pay. Baldness is a disease.
Pregnancy, on the other hand, is the natural state of women.'

Congress shall make no law . . . abridging freedom of speech, or of the press; or the right of the people peaceably to assemble, and to petition the Government for a redress of grievances*, *except when President Nixon comes to town*.

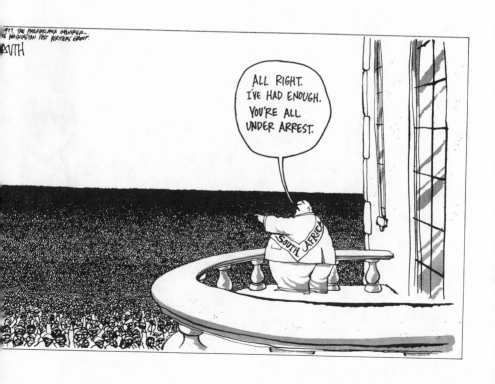

THIS WAS YOUR F.B.I.

GETTING ANGRY
SIX TIMES A WEEK

HUGH HAYNIE

"It's really tough to get angry six times a week," says Hugh Haynie, the editorial cartoonist for the Louisville *Courier-Journal*. But Haynie's been doing just that through the medium of his cartoons for over twenty-five years—getting angry at the abuses of the McCarthy era, at the agony of the civil rights struggle, at the pointless waste of the Vietnam war, at Watergate, and at our oftentimes puritanical society. Today, Haynie is still one of the strongest civil libertarian voices in the editorial pages of the Southern press and is still getting angry on a regular basis.

"Hugh Haynie is a transitional figure," his friend and colleague Draper Hill, editorial cartoonist of the Detroit *News*, says of him. "He is a bundle of paradoxes; a gracious, gregarious Virginia gentleman who answers his office phone with a ferocious 'YES?' guaranteed to put all but the hardiest intruders to instant flight. To him, the battles keep coming up one day at a time and the war is never over. Every cartoon is a new struggle to be fought each day between dawn and dusk. He has played a key role in the revitalization of the American editorial cartoon."

That role began while Haynie was still a student at the College of William and Mary in Williamsburg, Virginia, in the late forties when he was offered a part-time job on the staff of the Richmond *Times-Dispatch*. "When I first started out," Haynie recalls, "the most widely syndicated cartoonists were the ones who said absolutely nothing. They'd draw spring days, straw hats—the most innocuous things you could imagine. Herblock was just about the only person saying anything with great syndication. He took it from the other side of the coin and really hit with a hammer. As a result, it became more and more popular to make an honest-to-God statement." Greatly influenced by Herblock, Haynie went into cartooning with the self-proclaimed ideal of "being able to think like Herblock and draw like Walt Kelly [the creator of *Pogo*]."

In the early fifties, Haynie left Richmond to become the editorial cartoonist for the Greensboro, North Carolina *Daily News*, where his style matured. "My style changed in Greens-

128

boro for the simple reason of mechanics," says Haynie. "The Greensboro *News* was an excellent little paper, but mechanically it was abysmal. I had to get my cartoons in by two o'clock, so I needed a quick technique. The way I'd been drawing hadn't been quick at all. Consequently I lost my Herblockishness, and became Hayniesque, although I never seriously cultivated a style. It just sort of evolved." Haynie became the editorial cartoonist for the Louisville *Courier-Journal* in 1958, where he's labored ever since, turning out six cartoons a week. The Los Angeles *Times* syndicate began distributing his work nationally in the early sixties.

A Haynie cartoon is never something that one can overlook. It reaches out and startles the reader like a blast of cold air. Haynie himself admits that this is often his motive. "You must understand," he says, "that a cartoon is an *offensive* thing. It's a negative medium; rarely have I seen a good cartoon about anything positive. It also has an inherent weakness—you have to do it all in one shot. People must really understand what you're talking about before you start commenting."

When Haynie draws a civil liberties cartoon, his public doesn't have any trouble understanding what he's saying, although Haynie finds that he's drawing fewer civil liberties pieces than in the past. "Things just aren't as clearly defined today," he says. "The civil rights movement and the Vietnam war were very clear issues. The audience, pro and con, was right there, and they knew what you were talking about. Today's issues aren't always as sharp for me; there isn't always the same urgency. The CIA full-disclosure thing was hard, for example. I think we all agree that the CIA can't print everything it does in the newspapers, but what's happened so far is not what Carter promised in his campaign. I had very mixed emotions about the *Hustler* case, too. I wish we had a better client than Larry Flynt, but this thing still has to be nipped in the bud."

One issue that still remains sharp for Haynie, though, is the puritan character of American society. "Our society today isn't nearly as puritanical as the one in which I grew up," he says, "but it's still a pervasive element. I mean whenever I read my mail—even though I'm sure there are worse places—I get the distinct feeling that Louisville is the buckle on the Bible Belt."

Haynie would probably be surprised at the influence he's had on the new generation of editorial cartoonists. He is a man of quick wit, and his work always reflects his innate sense of humor.

"But, please continue, Mr. Carter...we're quite interested in your views on <u>international</u> arms control."

"But, mon Dieu! I HAD to release the PLO terrorist! They had me covered!"

"You may now genuflect, kiss the hem of my sari and thank me for giving you a free hand."

"Despite what you may have heard, I like a good dissenter, now 'n' then."

"It's just that dissenter doesn't like me."

"The court must understand that releasing these tapes would invade my privacy!"

"Okay, back in the water, lady! We've magnanimously
extended the time for your marathon swim!"

"I know . . . but, like you said y'self, Jimmy:
'Many things in life are unfair.' "

"Gee, fellas...since women are people, too, what say we let 'em join our club?"

"So you demand to call your editors? But, sir, we ARE now your editors!"

"Just when I thought I was finally rid of this..."

"...I got hit with a reverse punch."

SOMETIMES I LASH OUT AT BOTH SIDES

PAT OLIPHANT

P at Oliphant of the Washington *Star* doesn't like labels—especially when they're applied to him. While his work is often identified with liberal causes, he personally rebels against what he calls "extreme liberalism." He favors capital punishment, for example, and feels that school busing to achieve racial desegregation does more harm than good. Nevertheless, he supports the women's rights movement, thinks the FBI and CIA pose a very serious threat to civil liberties, and believes that our society's treatment of the elderly is scandalous. More often than not, though, his cartoons reflect his iconoclastic belief in "equal hostility to both sides of an issue."

"I always retain the right to change my mind," says Oliphant. "I'd rather not be categorized, and I resist that as much as possible. The ground I take in my drawings reflects how I feel that day toward a certain subject." About the only thing one can depend on from Oliphant is his wit.

Columnist Art Buchwald calls him "a threat to the American political system. His irreverent cartoons poke fun at the Establishment and raise grave doubts about the credibility of our leaders. The Oliphants of this world are dangerous because they make people think while they make them laugh. If I was in the White House, I'd lock him up and throw away the key." Oliphant's peculiar blend of humor and insight, combined with a unique drawing style, have made him one of the most influential cartoonists in the world today.

Born and raised in Adelaide on the southern coast of Australia, Oliphant attributes his cartooning career to a lucky break which, he says, transformed him from copy boy for the Adelaide *Advertiser* to their daily editorial cartoonist. He first visited the United States in 1959 on a round-the-world trip and decided this was the land of opportunity for him. "I liked this country, and saw great possibilities for establishing a new style of cartooning here," says Oliphant. "My influences were mostly British and Australian—artists like David Low—who were not too widely known in this country."

Contractual obligations kept Oliphant in Adelaide for five more years. Then, in 1964, he read in *Time* magazine that cartoonist Paul Conrad was leaving the Denver *Post* for the

Los Angeles *Times.* "I sent some examples of my work to the Denver *Post,*" he says "and they wrote back telling me to come over. I made the move in the space of one weekend. I stopped working in Adelaide on a Friday, and the following Monday I was on the job in Denver." Just three years later, in 1967, Oliphant was awarded the Pulitzer Prize. In 1975, he left Denver for the Washington *Star.* His work, syndicated by the Los Angeles *Times* Syndicate, appears in over 300 papers around the country.

An Oliphant cartoon is instantly recognizable. Typically, his characters are engaged in a burlesque of some current topic while a wise-cracking penguin, drawn in miniature, comments on the action from the lower-left- or right-hand corner of the drawing. It is this technique of counterpoint that makes Oliphant's work so distinct. "I'm sure this style must have been used before," he says, "but in my case it started as an original idea. I began using the penguin figure in Australia as a method of getting more than one idea into a cartoon. When you get more than one idea, you don't like to waste it. I chose the penguin for my everyman figure because it's an animal I like. There are lots of penguins in South Australia."

In the years since he came to America, Oliphant's style has been widely copied, almost to the point where many young cartoonists find it obligatory to insert some smart-aleck animal into a corner of their drawings. "I guess it's very gratifying to be copied," says Oliphant, "but I think stealing outright is carrying things too far. I'm flattered that I started a whole new style, but there's such a bandwagon tendency in these matters. I wish some young cartoonists would use someone else as an influence so that we get a little variety again."

Oliphant says that coming to America shortly after the Kennedy assassination, during the height of the civil rights movement and in the midst of the 1964 presidential campaign, was no great adjustment for him. "I really didn't feel any great trauma," he says. "I'd always been exposed to American reading matter, and, of course, America had always been of great interest to me."

Moving to Washington, where the grist for his mill is ground out, however, was another matter for Oliphant. "If you become immersed in Washington, it's easy to lose touch with the realities outside," he says. "I get out of Washington as often as I can." Right now, Oliphant sees the political realities of Washington in the doldrums. "After Nixon, Ford, and Watergate, the Carter regime has made this city a little boring," he says. "It's hard for me, as a cartoonist, to take on and develop a whole new cast of characters. If the people in Carter's administration become more widely known and recognizable, then I could caricature them more freely, but these are elusive people. You try to grab at what you can."

Bill Mauldin, no stranger to pioneering new techniques in cartooning, calls Oliphant's "a star of the first magnitude in the history of American cartooning."

'YOUR AUNT MURIEL IS SICK AND WISHES YOU'D WRITE... A BILL... YOUR NO-GOOD KID ON THE
EUROPE TOUR WANTS MONEY... ANOTHER BILL... POSTCARD FROM THE FIGBYS IN HAWAII!...JUNK...'

'CONGRATULATIONS, YOU HAVE QUALIFIED FOR A REBATE! BUT FIRST A FEW
QUESTIONS ABOUT YOUR POLITICAL AFFILIATIONS, SEX LIVES AND DRINKING HABITS...'

'BE THANKFUL, COMRADE, WE DON'T LIVE WITH A GOVERNMENT WHICH SPIES ON PEOPLE, PLANS ASSASSINATIONS, BUGS OFFICES, TAPS TELEPHONES, LIES TO US...'

'DON'T WORRY ABOUT A LITTLE PREGNANCY, LIEUTENANT— WE NO LONGER DISCRIMINATE AGAINST SUCH THINGS —— AND THAT'S ALL I WANT TO HEAR ABOUT IT, SERGEANT!'

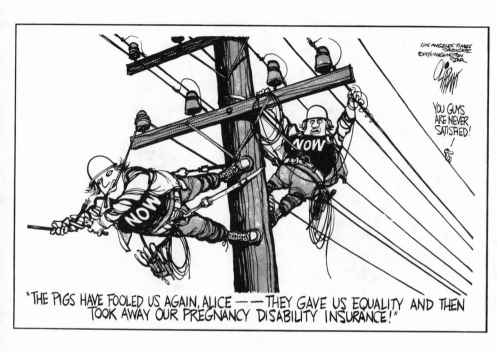

"THE PIGS HAVE FOOLED US AGAIN, ALICE——THEY GAVE US EQUALITY AND THEN TOOK AWAY OUR PREGNANCY DISABILITY INSURANCE!"

"LOOK THE OTHER WAY, PLEASE——I HAVE A FEW POLITICAL MURDERS TO ATTEND TO!"

THE WAYWARD BUS

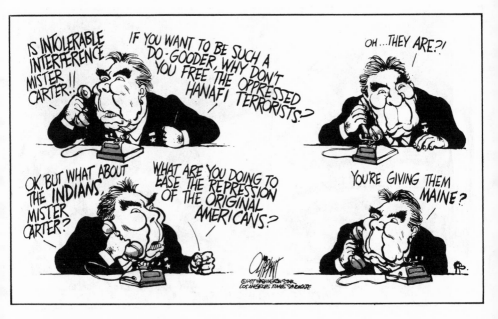

"RIOT CONTROL HAS CHANGED A LOT SINCE THE GOOD OLD NINETEEN SIXTIES, HASN'T IT?"

"BUT DON'T YOU KNOW A NICE NEIGHBORHOOD ABORTIONIST WHO COULD DO IT FOR YOU REASONABLY CHEAPLY?"

I TRY TO FORGET
THAT I'VE EVER READ
HISTORIES

DRAPER HILL

Ask almost any editorial cartoonist in the United States a question about the history of the profession, and the reply is bound to be, "Better go to Draper Hill for that." The daily pen-and-ink man for the Detroit *News* is, without a doubt, the resident historian in the small cadre of cartoonists, for his credentials are impeccable: Harvard B.A. magna cum laude, Fulbright scholar, and biographer of the eighteenth-century English caricaturist James Gillray.

In fact, his curriculum vitae would seem to suggest that Hill is the resident *intellectual* in the cartoonists' circle; when confronted with that accusation, however, he protests: "What a frightening thought!"

Draper Hill has not lost his sense of wry Yankee humor during his twenty-plus-year career; witticisms tumble from his lips. For instance, Hill's research into the reasons behind the inordinate number of southpaw cartoonists led him to wonder if it had "something to do with a lefty's habitual inclination to attack newspapers, magazines, books, problems, and other natural obstacles by starting at them from the rear." Trying to discern other bonds among his artistic fellows, he suspects that "cartoonists, unlike real people, never ask other cartoonists where they get their ideas from."

Yes, Draper Hill is a funny fellow. But inherent in his humor is a deep love for and knowledge of his profession, honed during years of serious study. He admits that the love came before the knowledge.

"I won't say I backed into cartooning through the historian's door, because I simply knew what I wanted to do and planned it from the start," says the forty-four-year-old Hill. "I *did* start, back in high school, fired by a not very original fascination with Thomas Nast, and moved on from there."

It was this fascination with Nast, coupled with his interest in Joseph Keppler of *Puck* and with the other pioneering popular artists of the late nineteenth century, that led Hill to favor political cartooning over two other artistic interests— sports cartooning and gag cartooning. He notes one other early experience, however, that helped him make up his mind.

"I was in the tenth grade, and I was fighting an election for class president with the reigning football captain," he recalls. "To my amazement, I turned the trick with a flood of placards and posters, each with a different—and obviously hand-drawn—cartoon. That was the first time I ever came up with a correlation between cartoons and the exercise of power."

The seed of a career goal planted, he entered Harvard in 1953 only to discover that the daily *Crimson* already had a first-rate cartoonist, an army veteran in his late twenties with three years of college yet to go. Undaunted, Hill turned to The Castle, the home of the *Harvard Lampoon*. Senior John Updike ("It was a little hard not to be awed stiff of him") was in charge of the humor magazine and had imbued it with the style of *The New Yorker*. Freshman Hill had found a niche.

"There were all kinds of drawings and posters hanging on the walls, from people who had been members, like *New Yorker* cartoonist Gluyas Williams, and from those who hadn't, like James Montgomery Flagg. For somebody fascinated with cartooning and caricature, like me, it had to turn into a historical orientation."

The *Lampoon* also succeeded in influencing Hill's style of political cartooning; he took up the captioned gag style favored by the magazine. To this day, Draper Hill might top off his daily offering with a Shakespearean quotation or other literary touch, which plays against the picture in unexpected and humorous ways.

Another major influence was the British satirical artist James Gillray, who died in 1815. Gillray developed the English school of political cartooning, the chief modern exponent of which was David Low. This Gillray-Low school was marked by a strong reliance on personal caricature and an impish fondness for irony and parody. Hill signed on as a devotee and pupil when, on a postgraduate tour of Europe, he called Low and met him for tea. That visit convinced the young artist to reject one job offered by a large electronics firm "to assume the role of assistant director in charge of making heavy electronic machinery sexually attractive." Instead he accepted a position as reporter and odd-job illustrator on the Quincy (Mass.) *Patriot-Ledger*. In 1960 he received a Fulbright grant to study art in London, during which time he began the serious study of Gillray. He subsequently produced three books on the man and his work.

Hill's combination of caricature and allusion make him stylistically unique among his compatriots. A quotation from

Lewis Carroll will amplify a picture of Griffin Bell as Humpty Dumpty and Jimmy Carter as Alice to illustrate a piece on racial quotas, or the Russian bear—a tired cartoon symbol—will look fresh when juxtaposed by Hill against the President as Brer Rabbit. Despite his frequent use of such techniques, Hill refuses to allow them to interfere with his reaching the general public.

"I try never to do anything which needs further reference, or which presumes any specific knowledge, unless perhaps it is how a nursery rhyme ends. But if I'm doing something out of Shakespeare, I would try to have it self-contained in a way that would banish the thought that I was condescending. It's a dangerous game to play."

Nevertheless, it's a danger he's willing to accept. "I just can't function without thinking of the cartoonist as a possible delivery system for grace notes that reward the reader who wants to stick around a bit longer that it takes to get the central point."

Readers were rewarded in Memphis for five years, following Hill's stint in Massachusetts, and the "cartoon-oriented readership" of that Southern city reciprocated by flocking to numerous public showings of the cartoonist's work. Then he moved to Detroit, where he recently passed his third anniversary.

Occasionally a little guy with dark hair and thick, black glasses, with a perplexed or troubled look on his face, will appear in a Draper Hill cartoon. This is the cartoonist playing Everyman with his own caricature. Hill claims he does it because "Mine is the most readily available mug on which I can suggest all the emotions I may need—stupidity, incompetence, complete bewilderment."

The face is currently registering these frowning emotions over a series of court cases that threaten to inhibit strong cartoonists. One is a successful libel suit brought by a Canadian official against a western Canadian cartoonist who depicted the official as unnecessarily cruel. The other is a domestic suit by Reddy Communication Inc. against the Environmental Action Foundation, which depicted RCI's friendly symbol, Reddy Kilowatt, in cartoons as a gambler and panhandler. Cartooning watchdog Hill is afraid of the chilling effect this might have on a profession that already has enough First Amendment inhibitions. "I worry about the future of the cartoon as philosophical troublemaker," he says, noting, "whether a cartoon is deeply dipped in whimsy or not, its value is as an irritant, as a lightning rod, as a catalyst."

The only thing that seems to oppress him heavily, though, is the weight of his own knowledge—the perennial problem of the scholar. "Every morning," laments Hill, "I just try to forget that I have ever read a history, or looked at thousands of cartoons."

Ah, but he has, and the results of Draper Hill's studies are evident every day in the Detroit *News*. We're all the better for it.

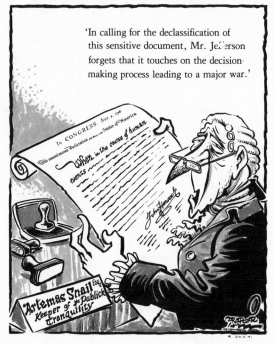

'In calling for the declassification of this sensitive document, Mr. Jefferson forgets that it touches on the decision-making process leading to a major war.'

"Get rid of it..."

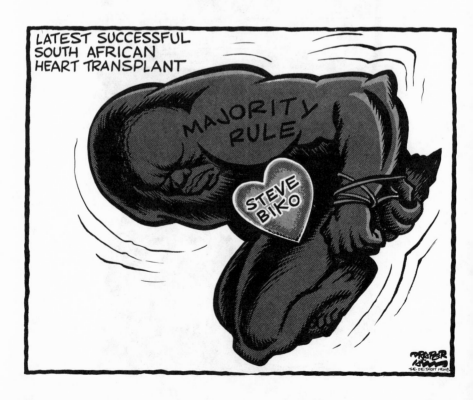

"MIND IF I POKE AROUND?"